Transforming Leader Paradigms

Transforming Leader Paradigms

Evolve from Blanket Solutions to Problem Solving for Complexity

James E. Luckman
Olga Flory

CRC Press
Taylor & Francis Group
Boca Raton London New York

CRC Press is an imprint of the
Taylor & Francis Group, an **informa** business

First edition published in 2019
by Routledge/Productivity Press
52 Vanderbilt Avenue, 11th Floor New York, NY 10017
2 Park Square, Milton Park, Abingdon, Oxon OX14 4RN, UK

© 2019 by James E. Luckman and Olga Flory

Routledge/Productivity Press is an imprint of Taylor & Francis Group, an Informa business

No claim to original U.S. Government works

Printed on acid-free paper

International Standard Book Number-13: 978-0-367-13930-8 (Hardback)

International Standard Book Number-13: 978-0-429-02925-7 (eBook)

**Visit the Taylor & Francis Web site at
http://www.taylorandfrancis.com**

Contents

Preface

Dear Reader,

By picking up this book, you probably already know that organizations today are dealing with very complex, interdependent problems. The marketplace, customer expectations, and employee demands are changing at accelerated rates, requiring a more adaptable management approach.

You are likely wondering about your role in all of this. Maybe you are thinking, "There must be a better way to lead."

You may have observed that in this new context, many leaders randomly throw hoped-for solutions at their organization without clearly defining problems. Over the past few decades, management fad programs, driven by consultants, popular books, and business schools, have been adopted as primary approaches for making improvements. Once fad programs or blanket solutions are adopted, they create overlap, confusion, and overburden. Most importantly, they become deeply embedded in the organizational practices and become a part of the company culture. Unfortunately, they don't always help address real business problems.

Another common practice you may have observed is how leadership teams tend to roll out blanket solutions throwing money, people, and/or other resources at a problem without understanding its root cause. Have you moved your manufacturing offshore? Have you had broad headcount reductions? Have you pursued new acquisitions? Have you reorganized? Have you purchased costly new IT systems? Have you sold off your underperforming businesses? Have you moved software development to India?

It is time for a new kind of leadership altogether.

We first began thinking deeply about this in 2008, while working at The Lean Enterprise Institute. Jim, formerly an executive in several U.S. companies, supported LEI as a faculty member and a consultant. Olga, who spent many years as a senior leader in companies ranging from startups to global corporations in the U.S. and abroad, ran LEI's education "value stream." In this line of work, we had an opportunity to meet with folks from all kinds of organizations and industries from all over the globe who, despite their diversity, seemed to have something in common: a deep disappointment in the results of their efforts to build a new organizational culture, and a persistent curiosity about the role of leaders in driving meaningful change.

We decided to create a realistic business simulation to help leaders—through participation in a problem-solving exercise—understand their role in changing the culture of their organizations. The reason we used problem solving as a framework for learning was that we shared a belief about the linkage between organizational culture and the leadership approach to solving organizational problems. We used a definition of culture suggested by Edgar Schein: *"Culture is a pattern of shared basic assumptions that the group learned as it solved its problems of external adaptation and internal integration."* Instead of focusing on the grand task of culture transformation, we aimed to give participants an opportunity to experience the consequences of their current leadership practices and introduce them to leadership thinking needed for a different kind of more effective problem solving.

In the first part of this workshop, participants engaged in experiential learning by participating in a business simulation, working as a leadership team of a company with several lines of business and a variety of services and products. Then we facilitated several rounds of deep reflection so they could see the impacts of their actions on their ability to solve business problems in collaboration with others.

In the nine years since the launch of the program, we have observed hundreds of workshop participants go through the process of self-discovery as they attempted to solve problems inside the simulation. They recognized their underdeveloped skills and learned how to practice building these skills when they returned to their home organizations. They learned how to structure small experiments to practice skill building for themselves and their teams.

What we weren't prepared for was the learning that we, designers and facilitators, were getting out of this experience! Now, after many years of observing leaders in the simulation and in their organizations, we want to share what we have learned about leadership practices that support the ability of organizations to adapt to the demands of this complex and rapidly changing world. We hope that this book will help you think about how you approach change and decide what you need to change *about yourself* to maximize your personal effectiveness—through the organizational transformation process and beyond.

We intend for this book to assist you in leading a carefully crafted evolution for building an adaptable, energetic organization that is great at solving problems. We draw on *neuroscience, complexity science, Gestalt theory, and our own observations* to offer a new way of working that allows leaders to facilitate meaningful change in complex organizations.

We invite you to join us on a journey of self-discovery and deliberate practice for developing leadership skills needed to lead your organization through a bold cultural transformation. We'll talk about culture change but won't focus directly on changing the culture. Instead, we will aim to help you transform your own personal thinking and actions to influence the thinking and actions of your organization. We hope you will find this book useful in helping you navigate through the challenges you and your company face daily and prepare you to deal with new problems of added complexity and magnitude.

There is a better way to lead change in your organization.

Let's get started.

Acknowledgments

This book wouldn't be written without the support and contribution from many people. We want to express our deepest appreciation to:

Michael Sinocchi, editor at Taylor and Francis Group, for his belief in our vision for the book from day one, and his continued support throughout the process — from the first draft chapter to the publication;

Alexis Schroeder, who courageously took the role of our development editor and helped shape the flow of content, and bring individual chapters into a coherent manuscript;

Cia Ochsenbein, for taking our amateurish PowerPoint graphics and converting them into beautiful professional images;

Kirk Paluska, Tom Foco, and Margie Hagene, who helped design and facilitate the Transformational Leadership Program at the Lean Enterprise Institute, which became the source of many concepts and ideas introduced in this book;

Jim Womack and Helen Zak, for all the emotional and financial support they provided to the group of inexperienced designers that allowed the program to come to life;

Mike Emery, Kimberly Hannon, Sister Paula Marie Buley, Adrian Verduzco, and Karl Ohaus, for sharing their transformation stories and opening up about the challenges they faced as leaders when they realized they needed to fundamentally change their leadership styles;

Hundreds of attendees of the Transformational Leadership Program for their openness, willingness to try new leadership approaches and feedback that allowed us to continuously improve the program and learn throughout the process.

I (Olga) would like to thank my husband Tom for his steady belief in me, his readiness to be the sounding board for our ideas and concerns, and the unwavering enthusiasm about the outcomes of this undertaking, even when Jim and I weren't that sure we were going to get it done. Also, special thanks to my son Nikita who, right at the time when we started working on the book, signed up with the U.S. Marine Corp. Seeing how hard he trained to get himself ready for the boot camp was the best motivation to stay focused on this project.

I (Jim) want to thank my partners of the Lean Transformations Group who tirelessly emphasize learning and creating knowledge in their engagements with clients. Tom Shuker takes difficult problems and creates practical and actionable next steps. Karl Ohaus creates a respectful and treasured connection with his clients. David Verble models the highest level of curiosity and is never satisfied with what we think we understand about problem situations. Judy Worth, who recently retired from our group, was the primary writer of our book "Perfoecting Patient Journeys" and helped us make are messages more understandable.

Finally, I want to thank my two daughters, Elizabeth and Vanessa, who have been an important part of expanding my thinking through their insight, understanding, and challenging conversations. They encouraged me to look through different lenses to clarify my thoughts during the process of writing the book. Last, but not least, I want to thank my wife, Vikki, for her ongoing support, down to earth advice, and her ability to make me laugh when I needed to take a break from writing.

About the Authors

James E. (Jim) Luckman loves solving big problems. An engineer by training, he has expanded beyond his technical problem-solving expertise to solving complex social problems in organizations. He works with diverse companies by coaching leaders on how to transform their organizations to a culture of energized problem solvers.

Jim has dedicated his life to problem solving with over 30 years in industry as an engineer and leader, and 17 years in professional services as a coach. He has had the unique experience of leading three separate Lean transformations in leadership roles: as a Plant Manager, as a Director of a Research and Development Center, and as a CEO of a small start-up company. In his coaching role, he has engaged with hundreds of companies and organizational function in a wide variety of industries (e.g. finance, food products, automotive, government, insurance, construction, health care, and universities). Each coaching engagement has generated improved organizational performance and increased employee enthusiasm and sense of responsibility for solving problems.

Jim is a founding partner of The Lean Transformations Group, a consulting group created in 2006 focused on building problem-solving capabilities in companies. The business partners of the Lean Transformation Group have been dedicated to developing and innovating an intervention methodology that can be used in all industries to engage the workforce to more effectively and efficiently solve problems. The organizations who have benefited from this intervention have achieved improved business results through more engaged employees.

Jim is a faculty member of the Lean Enterprise Institute. He has published articles on Lean leadership and is a co-author of two books, *Mapping to See* and *Perfecting Patient Journeys* which was a recipient of the Shingo Research and Professional Publication Award. He has been a speaker at the annual Lean Enterprise Transformation Summit and The Philosophy of Management Conference. Jim has a B.S. in Electrical Engineering from Tri-State University and an M.S. in Computer Engineering from Case Western Reserve University. Jim has a wife, Victoria, two daughters, Elizabeth and Vanessa, and a granddaughter, Eleanor. Jim can be contacted at jluckman@lean-transform.com.

Olga Flory A transplant from Siberia, Olga has lived through Russian Federation's transition from the Soviet-style economy to the free market, and had a unique opportunity to support the development of the first generation of business leaders in that country.

Throughout her career, she held executive and senior leadership positions at startups and Fortune 100 companies in industries ranging from manufacturing to sales and distribution, construction, finance, insurance, and consulting. In her quest to find the secret to great leadership, she studied the effects of leadership behaviors on people and organizations in a wide variety of companies with a broad range of business practices, around the globe. Converting her observations into learning interventions, she helps leaders develop mindsets and behaviors that support their ability to build high-performing and continuously improving organizations. In her coaching engagements, she focuses on the development of critical leadership competencies that allow leaders to create the environment of trust, respect, and mutual accountability.

Olga holds a Master's degree in Education and Linguistics from the State Pedagogical University, Krasnoyarsk, Russia, and a Brain-Based Coaching certification by The NeuroLeadership Institute, New York, New York.

Olga and her husband, Tom, live in Leominster, Massachusetts. Her son, Nikita, serves in the United States Marine Corps. Olga can be reached at oflory01@gmail.com.

Introduction

"The greatest danger in times of turbulence is not the turbulence — it is to act with yesterday's logic."

Peter Drucker

This book is for leaders who want to guide their organization to new, extraordinary levels of performance and leaders who have made the deliberate choice to examine their own behaviors and practices in order to do so. This is not a book about how to implement a change initiative; it is a book about what leadership means today, given what we know about the complex systems we live and work in, the way organizations work, and how people learn.

We continue to observe key trends in "change initiatives." First, most change initiatives do not produce the expected performance improvement. Second, the role leaders take is not different from their current model they habitually use on all the active initiatives. They do not recognize that a deep change, one that alters the culture of an organization, requires a completely different leadership model. Third, the new reality is that we live in a turbulent, unpredictable world that requires significant change to the way teams work and organizations function. Making this type of holistic organizational change means we need a new model of leadership.

A GLANCE AT TWO DRAMATICALLY DIFFERENT PARADIGMS

This book introduces two dominant paradigms—*"Imposing Blanket Solutions"* and *"Problem Solving for Complexity"*—that influence an organizational approach to problem solving and, as a result, shape very different cultures. We are suggesting that you adopt the problem solving paradigm that acknowledges the complexity of the world we live in and encourages you to work with and inside *complex adaptive systems*. The new leadership model that is shaped by this new paradigm is based on the realization that any organization is a complex adaptive system in itself, capable of self-organizing to solve problems using a systems approach supported by respectful and trusting human relationships. Why? Today's management systems need to be capable of bringing people together to address *complex, unpredictable,* and *interdependent* problems and solve them by identifying and addressing interdependent causes of such problems.

The two paradigms we introduce in this book are based on a set of contrasting (and almost always unquestioned) assumptions.

One paradigm shapes the culture of hierarchical dominance, which suppresses initiative, where problem solving is the privilege of some specifically designated individuals. Problems are typically solved by a quick application of solutions that target the symptoms of problems, not their root causes. This paradigm assumes predictability and the ability to control outcomes. All of the parts in the system—people, functions, organizational systems, and practices—can be controlled and replaced as if everything is independent. Imposing Blanket Solutions is not good at helping you and your organization address problems in today's world.

The other contrasting paradigm, Problem Solving for Complexity, views organizations not as a simple composition of individual parts but rather as complex adaptive systems. In this system, the ability of an organization to continuously evolve, grow, and improve the flow of value to the customer results not from top-down leadership decisions but from the engagement of all employees into daily experimentation and learning. To help employees transition to this new paradigm and engage in deep learning, trust and respect are essential. Leaders must demonstrate both day-in-day-out in order to create the psychological safety that is required for meaningful change. A nurturing environment that supports employee learning and encourages their daily contributions to the continuous improvement of work, systems, and processes is what leads to higher performance.

As a leader looking to build an effective culture, you need to understand which assumptions, both individual and organizational, currently influence the culture of your company and learn how to transition to a new set of assumptions if you agree that the current ones are flawed. By understanding these assumptions and applying deliberate practice, we see leaders move their organization from the paradigm of Imposing

Blanket Solutions to the much more effective paradigm of Problem Solving for Complexity.

QUESTIONING THE MOST POPULAR IDEAS ABOUT LEADERSHIP

Most of the current leadership and management ideas, we believe, come from a solutions-oriented perspective centering around the all-knowing, heroic leader. This leader defines outcomes and rolls out a structured "change program" with an expectation that if the outcomes are clear and the program structure is well defined, the organization will follow suit. This always causes resistance from team members. As a result, change leaders direct most of their efforts to minimize the resistance instead of focusing on what is really important: engaging team members in a more organic change process to solve problems that matter to the organization and to the customer. This process takes into consideration organizational complexity and is based on the understanding of how complex adaptive systems work.

But if you take a quick look at the top ten leadership books on Amazon, we would bet that most if not all of them reinforce the top-down, hyper-individualist perspective, focusing on the leader outside of the organizational context. Recent publications by John Maxwell and Simon Sinek, helpful as they may be, still reinforce these basic ideas. You may ask why publishers think their customer wants these types of books. Perhaps because it is easier to put our stock in the all-knowing, charismatic leader than to admit that no leader can single-handedly control outcomes and the process for delivering them.

Most leadership books suggest solutions for leaders. They have a common theme of describing characteristics of successful leaders, with an unquestioned assumption that these characteristics need to be emulated. The problem is that a simple imitation of leadership behaviors by team members is insufficient for creating a sustainable change. What popular books on leadership don't adequately address is how leaders need to work with the rest of the organization to accomplish a paradigm shift from Imposing Blanket Solutions to Problem Solving for Complexity and support the emergence of the new culture. We believe organizations today need both strong executive leadership *and* the "working with" approach.

STANDING ON THE SHOULDERS OF LEAN GIANTS

Our introduction to Problem Solving for Complexity came as a result of our study and personal practice of Lean. Together, the two of us have spent close to 40 years learning and teaching in the Lean community. As a result, we totally embrace the basic principles of Lean but go beyond Lean in some very specific ways.

For folks who are unfamiliar with Lean, in *Lean Thinking* (1996), James P. Womack and Daniel T. Jones shared their observations of Toyota and the Toyota Production System and defined the five principles that they called Lean:

1. Specify value from the standpoint of the end customer by product family.
2. Identify all the steps in the value stream for each product family, eliminating whenever possible those steps that do not create value.
3. Make the value-creating steps occur in tight sequence so the product will flow smoothly toward the customer.
4. As flow is introduced, let customers pull value from the next upstream activity.
5. As value is specified, value streams are identified, wasted steps are removed, and flow and pull are introduced, begin the process again and continue it until a state of perfection is reached in which perfect value is created with no waste.

The very first of these principles, *Specify value from the standpoint of the end customer by product family*, creates clarity of the purpose for the organization. Identifying the external customers and where and how your organization delivers value provides team alignment and simplicity. Once this purpose is understood and embraced, all parts of the organization can work to make improvements toward this purpose. Team members in Lean organizations focus on creating customer value with less waste. They understand themselves to be part of a value-creating process that crosses all organizational boundaries to serve the end customer.

You might imagine that since the release of *Lean Thinking*, thousands of companies around the globe have tried to transform their businesses into the Lean enterprise. Unfortunately, many Lean efforts start with a bang but lose energy over time and then have problems with sustainability. According to a 2015 McKinsey report, over 70% of all transformation efforts fail. We don't have specific data on Lean transformations but, based on our observations, we believe that their success rate is similarly disappointing. Why? We observe a few reasons for this.

We believe most Lean transformations tend to focus on the deployment of *tools* which were invented by Toyota for Toyota, as countermeasures to business problems that Toyota faced and needed to deal with at different stages of its history. *Standardized work, 5S, valuestream maps, heijunka boards, kanban, supermarket,* and so on... These are the tools that Toyota developed and introduced to support the ability of its team members to solve problems. Every day, every hour, every minute.

Applying these tools with a fad mentality in a totally different business and cultural context, as part of a general "Lean toolbox," with little or no connection to specific problems that companies face, shifts organizational focus from people solving problems using the tools to how many tools have been implemented and how many people have used them. Typically, these tools are used in addition to other existing tools and practices, which almost always create unnecessary confusion and extra work.

Furthermore, focusing on the tools, Lean practitioners too often fail to address the social side of Lean transformations, that is, how leaders need to build respectful connections with people to encourage them to bring up problems and create the environment for effective problem solving. People are more naturally afraid to openly talk about problems. If they are not exposing problems, they cannot make improvements.

If you visit "Lean" companies, you will probably see teams meeting in front of huddle boards, or conducting problem-solving meetings where they use A3 storyboards. You may even see leaders on process walks (a commonly used term for the "go-and-see" practice pioneered by Toyota managers) that they take according to their standard calendars. All of this will be impressive at first. But if you slow down and take a closer look, you will realize that often they are simply going through the motions. They may be following new *rituals* but their *thinking* hasn't really changed, which is why problem-solving meetings end with quick solutions, huddle conversations are about firefighting, and process walks are either used for "shaking hands and kissing babies," or to tell team members how to do their jobs. Many leaders think they are being Lean, but they aren't truly listening to and working with and alongside their team members.

To be clear, we have observed the Lean practice in a number of organizations that have achieved both significantly improved performance and greater employee engagement and enthusiasm. All these organizations have something in common: leadership practices and behaviors that support the ability of employees to identify and solve problems turning every problem-solving effort into a learning experience that is shared with the rest of the organization so that others can benefit from it.

While these organizations have learned some great things from Lean thinking and practice, in the majority of companies that have attempted to transform their organizations to the Lean enterprise, the implementation continues to have limited benefits because leaders and Lean practitioners do not make an effort to comprehend their existing paradigm of Imposing Blanket Solutions. While Lean started as a movement to attempt at a paradigm shift, unfortunately, it has not achieved the complete shift to the Problem Solving for Complexity culture in most companies.

We offer these hard lessons learned on Lean because Lean thinking has taught us to bring a spirit of inquiry to everything we do, and we know Lean thinking and practice and complexity theory need each other. We've had many "a-ha" moments over the years through our work in the Lean community and in other contexts, and this book is a result of those moments. But we believe we have learned lessons that go beyond Lean.

We have written this book to build upon Lean to help leaders create culture change in the following ways:

- We offer a way to overcome the problems of implementation of Lean. This book approaches change by describing a leader approach to culture change instead of applying tools through a program approach.
- We emphasize the need for adaptability, approaching change by embracing the characteristics of complex adaptive systems. Teams

are created for adaptability and working together at correcting complex problems.

- We recognize the need for creating a new relationship between supervisor and direct report that overcomes the hierarchy bias by acknowledging both are learning new skills that enable culture change. We suggest that to make culture change, all people, regardless of their position, are learning together and should respect each other as if they are co-learners.

- We suggest a learning model that uses five assumptions of culture to manage the learning for transforming paradigms. Starting with the awareness and understanding of the assumptions that support the paradigm, we use a method of learning that reflects on five basic assumptions.

- We encourage all participants in the culture change process to look for the emergent characteristics that are a result of valuing the diversity of thinking among the group. This book emphasizes "seeing and learning together" as the key for taking advantage of different viewpoints in addressing system problems.

The book starts with "*Awakening,*" a call to action that helps leaders start on a path toward change. Included in this section is a description of the new model for leaders that is in alignment with a new complex system worldview. Also, we describe the a-ha moments leaders have experienced to initiate their change journey.

The second part, "*Awareness,*" introduces three foundational concepts that, we think, can help you understand the challenges of your unique leadership journey.

Part three is all about "Action". We discuss actions leaders can take to move organizations from Imposing Blanket Solutions to Problem Solving for Complexity: building a framework for solving value-stream problems, supporting social interactions that create environments of respect and safety, and helping team members learn through problem-solving efforts.

In "Actualization", we discuss how you can start building your individual leadership skills so that the whole organization gets inspired to build skills needed for a total transformation. We include a chapter with the stories of leaders who have taken the leap toward becoming introspective role models for their teams.

The final chapter is the "Deep Dive". It is for those of you who want to learn as you go and reflect on how this applies to your personal situation. In it, you will find a list of questions for reflection and a few recommendations for further reading for each chapter. As you finish each chapter, you can go here to expand your understanding of the content and how it applies to you.

What this book is not is a magic bullet, nor is it a solution that you can simply apply to your organization. Instead, we guide you through a problem-solving approach, a process you can use to lead your organization to be aligned with a new paradigm. It helps you start from your current condition and move to your newly defined future. The approach to leadership that we introduce requires a lot of discipline and persistence on the part of the leader—you! How long it takes is hard to estimate because each organization is different. The starting point, the size of the organization, and the current demands of the organization all have significant influence on the time it takes to see results and sustainability.

We have seen some leaders of stand-alone organizations, where they have the authority and responsibility for their change effort, make significant sustainable culture change in less than a year. We have also seen large, complex, global organizations have much difficulty and take many years to realize the benefits of a new culture. For a large organization, achieving common understanding across many separate organizations makes it difficult to change policies and procedures to support the new culture. Yet, since culture change is about engaging people in effective problem solving, local units can change quickly if leaders are intentional about their own actions. And if you stay on course, you end up with a culture that will not only help your company survive through external and/or internal turmoil but enjoy steady long-term prosperity.

If you begin experimenting with a problem-solving mindset, you will create *many* opportunities for personal awakenings. Our hope is that by reading this book, you will discover many new ideas for learning how to break your own leadership habits while helping your organization learn how to learn.

Part 1

Awakening

When we (Olga and Jim) sat down to reflect on what we've learned about leadership during the times of change, there was quite a bit of material to mull over and discern. What was clear to us was that it all starts with an awakening of sorts ... a sense that what came before was before, and the future will never be the same. There is no going back (which means there is no going back to our old leadership habits either)!

We've each experienced awakening ourselves and witnessed it plenty of times in others. It helped us recognize that the leader's awakening is a synergistic two-way process and experience. Its external focus is about how one's leadership style and practice affect relationships with others, and the other is the ongoing internal reflection, the relationship to one's self. The external focus is cognitive; it looks outside you and describes the world and conditions needing to be addressed and, then, how leadership needs to change to address those conditions. We'll focus on this in Chapter 1, "*The New Role of Leadership.*" The second component of awakening is something that happens inside your unconscious self. You cannot control it. It grows within you and redefines who you are. What emerges is the real you, the you that now sees the world as an interconnected whole where you are creating something new and important for others, with others. We'll talk more about this in Chapter 2, "*From a Caterpillar to a Butterfly.*" Since this new you emerges from within your unconscious mind, you cannot fully understand what is happening; it just happens. Some people call this a soul awakening.

In the first chapter, we dig into the reasons a new leadership is needed in the context of the world today. We offer some ideas about leadership theories and share with you our vision for creating a culture that not only emerges under your leadership but goes well beyond your time at your company. The second chapter covers the energy that rises from within you where you begin to act with a greater purpose. You create closer connections with others and build the strength to leave your current ordinary world and venture into the unknown. This is where you shed your skin and have a metamorphosis into a new you. You transform yourself, just like a caterpillar transforms into a butterfly.

This *transformed you* will guide you as you journey into the new unknown world.

1

The New Role of the Leader

"We keep moving forward, opening new doors, and doing new things, because we're curious and curiosity keeps leading us down new paths."
Walt Disney

You are a leader. Congratulations! You likely made it to your current position through your focus, hard work, and dedication, not to mention your set of highly developed skills.

How do the people who work with you describe you? Are you a person who can quickly work through complex issues, make decisions, and set a clear direction? Maybe you are the "go-to" person to develop a long-term vision and establish business strategies due to your passion and ability to thoroughly analyze the market, competitors, and suppliers. Maybe you are the best at mobilizing the right resources to solve problems. Or perhaps you are a master change agent who understands what it takes to move your team to new performance levels.

Whatever people think about you, you have worked hard at developing your unique skill set over time. You have reached a level of excellence that is appreciated by your superiors, peers, and employees. And depending on your specific title—CEO, Director, VP, General Manager, and so on—your skills are some of the best for your position. You are highly respected for both your leadership and your status in the corporate hierarchy. And, like any good leader, you always aim to make your team successful. Over time, you have probably implemented programs and initiatives with the intention to build a strong, healthy, positive culture to help propel your team forward. But, our guess is, something is still bothering you.

Let's think together. This is because there is still a problem. You have developed skills to excel inside your existing management system, which is likely buried in a mental and cultural paradigm that currently dominates your organizational thinking and behaviors. And something about this paradigm is not helping you meet your current business challenges. It is just getting harder to get things done.

A BRAND-NEW WORLD

To say our world today is "fast-paced" and everything seems to be speeding up is a massive understatement. Consider how the way we receive news has changed, how we are bombarded by instant messaging, and how our businesses now get customer feedback on social media platforms like Facebook. Your leadership philosophy, which influences the way your team performs its work, may have been fine 50 years or even a decade ago, but today it no longer can keep up. Think about how just the size of your email inbox has grown. The speed of communications and increasing level of noise have made it difficult for us to know and decide what is important. It's impossible to respond to every email and consider every new piece of information coming your way.

Closely related to the increased speed of communications, is the connectedness of everything in our world. Almost every part of every system influences the other. This is called *interdependence*, and it is why business problems (or any problems, really) cannot be solved with simple cause-and-effect thinking. Solving problems now requires many people, with different perspectives, working together to influence and shift complex interdependent processes. Over the past two decades, we have seen the problems and opportunities related to interdependencies at nearly every company we have visited.

Along with complexity and interdependencies comes uncertainty. You might say uncertainty is what defines our world today. More and more events that we can neither predict nor prevent happen on a daily basis. Consider the impact of 9/11, the financial crisis of 2008, and more recently, Brexit. These were all significant disruptions that most people didn't see coming. Besides diverting actions to correcting for these disruptions, these events each caused massive re-thinking about what to do after things settled down.

The workplace today experiences similar disruptions, whether leaders acknowledge them and face them head-on or not. Customers decide to change suppliers because of something they see on Twitter ... Mergers result in restructuring ... Changes in the volatile stock market cause leaders to take drastic actions to maintain stability ... Learning how to respond rapidly and wisely to these kinds of disruptions is simply a required feature for companies to survive, let alone thrive.

A BRAND-NEW MANAGEMENT PHILOSOPHY?

Most companies have a management philosophy that is at least a half-century behind today's reality. Most leaders, through no fault of their own, are still practicing these outdated leadership skills, even though these skills no longer work to address the problems we see today.

Here are some questions for you to ponder.

Who does the thinking and who is doing the work?

In many companies, the management philosophy is still based on the concept of separating *thinking* from *doing*. Leaders establish strategies, roll them out, expect their people to accept the directives, and work toward accomplishing the goals. This is what is called a command-and-control management, and sadly, it is still far too common today.

Are the processes static and controllable or are they dynamic and adaptive?

Some processes are more static, stable, and transactional, meaning they can be controlled. Others are much more dynamic and therefore unstable. For example, in many manufacturing operations, some sequential processes where one step leads to another do not change much. However, in other functions, primarily in product development and sales, processes are more variable because they create *knowledge*, not parts, and require adaptability and speed. "Operators" in these departments need significant continuous change and re-adjustment. One size does not fit all and, yet, many leadership practices were developed for static and controllable processes. Leaders need to become aware of these differences and determine the best way to engage their team members and guide the interactions between them.

How many millennials are among your company employees and what do you notice about their approach to work?

Millennials bring a different focus to your workplace these days. They may not be as willing to accept the current leadership model as other employees have. They tend to prioritize values, ethics, and flexibility and, as a result, they may expect more diversity and inclusion. They will challenge previously established policies, and you will need to adjust to their demands. You can see this as a problem or an opportunity ... an evolution ... a sign of the times.

What is the global footprint of your business?

Geographically separated teams have additional communication needs to deliver customer value. How often and how effectively they communicate will have a significant impact on your business. "Handoffs" are a problem everywhere, even when people sit next to each other, but these problems are more amplified by long distance.

A NEW ENERGETIC APPROACH TO "EMPLOYEE ENGAGEMENT"

If we want people to feel capable of making decisions and taking problem-solving actions that are important to the business, then we need to trust that they care about the business. This means we need to go beyond the business jargon and think seriously about what *"employee engagement"* looks and feels like. According to Keven Kruse, a *New York Times* best-selling author, "Employee engagement" is the *"emotional commitment* an employee has to the organization and its goals, resulting in the use of *discretionary effort."* Recent studies have discovered that only 30% of employees are engaged in their work. Keven has created a master list of 32 research findings about the impact of employee engagement, which include:

- Companies with high employee engagement scores had **twice the customer loyalty**
- Percent of industry net **sales increased by 300%** in a large manufacturing company

- A Fortune 100 manufacturing company reduced quality errors from **5,658** parts per million to **52** parts per million.
- Business units in the **bottom quartile averaged 62% more accidents**
- Employees with lower engagement **are four times more likely to leave**
- Organizations with highly engaged employees achieve **twice the annual net income**

We like these stats because they remind us that increasing employee engagement is key to improving company performance. But, from experience, we know that this really only works if it is done in a way that is integrated with a leadership team's approach to creating a culture that focuses on solving business problems. If you attempt to address the issue of employee engagement as a separate initiative, then it will surely be seen by employees as just another "fad program."

How do you increase engagement in a brand-new leadership and management context? To answer this question, let's review some theories of leadership in practice today.

According to **Transactional Leadership Theory**, leaders need to be highly action and results focused. They spend most of their time reviewing checklists of tasks and looking at charts of results. It is the traditional "carrot and stick" approach. Reward and punishment are based on the ability to achieve results. Leadership behaviors demonstrate low trust and low respect for employees.

Leader–Member Exchange (LMX) Theory in comparison is less focused on results and more focused on high-quality social connections. Team members are encouraged to take on more responsibility and make more decisions. According to this theory, greater performance results from better social connections.

Transformational Leadership Theory takes LMX Theory to a higher level by adding more inspiration, vision, and thoughtfulness. Leaders who are transformative in their approach adopt the theory of LMX that better social connections lead to better performance. They also focus on aligning their organization to a larger vision and believe that they need to be more inspirational.

Every theory identifies core leadership skills in support of its model. For example, if your company is aligned with the Transactional Leadership Theory, you likely have highly developed skills that help you focus on results. Both LMX and Transformational Leadership, on the other hand, emphasize interpersonal growth and quality social connections, which requires leaders to have a different set of skills.

Rather than invest in special leadership training programs though, we believe there is a better way to achieve higher levels of engagement. This is when leaders and team members engage in the deliberate practice of working collaboratively to solve real business problems, in the here-and-now. Skill development in this model takes place in a real-time practice field while working alongside your employees at solving complex problems. You are in an active role as a leader, guiding your company, business unit, and/or team to create and use a more effective problem-solving process. Your team members learn together as you all adapt to the rapidly changing conditions and challenges of your business. As you are developing your own skills and helping your employees learn, you gradually transition your organization to a Problem Solving for Complexity Culture. We'll cover this concept of on-the-job experimentation and learning in more detail in later chapters.

MORE LIKE WALT DISNEY, LESS LIKE JACK WELCH

When Jack Welch retired as CEO of GE in 2001, after 20 years of extraordinary results, the company's value had risen 4000%. Revenues increased from $25 billion to $130 billion, profits grew ten-fold to $15 billion, and market capitalization grew by a multiple of 30 to an impressive $400 million. He initiated many new management practices during his tenure, and because of GE's successes, many other companies adopted these practices. The "Jack Welch influence" spread far beyond the walls of GE. In 1999, Fortune Magazine described Jack Welch as the best manager of the 20th century. He certainly was the most influential leader of his generation.

But what happened to GE after Welch retired? Did the successes continue? In 2017, 16 years after Jeff Immelt replaced Jack as CEO, GE was in a very different place. One indicator, GE stock price, was down 25% while the S&P had a 59% rise. Other large companies had successes while GE dropped. Honeywell doubled, Danaher tripled, and United Technologies had a 67% increase.

Was the problem Welch, or was it Immelt? Or ... was it too complex a problem situation to pin on one person? Welch did have different challenges than Immelt. During Immelt's time as CEO, he was faced with 9/11, the financial meltdown, and the tech bubble. But other companies experienced the same market disturbances, and they gained while GE declined. Leaders have a major influence on company performance, but they also are responsible for creating the culture necessary to respond to the world we live in. Did Welch leave behind a culture that would continue growing, developing, and making continuous improvements after his departure? It's hard to say. Leaders should be reflective about how they impact the culture and if that culture can continue. The question before leaders needs to be, "What happens *after* I leave?"

In contrast, Walt Disney was a dreamer. His leadership style was aligned with the Transformational Leadership Theory. He wanted to create something beyond himself for other people and build high-quality social connections with his employees. Like most dreamers, he started with many setbacks, failures, and near financial ruin. His ongoing vision and persistence (and perhaps a little luck) helped him overcome his setbacks, one problem at a time. Today, Disney stock price, adjusted for many splits since Walt's death in 1967, has grown from $.32 to $110 per share. Disney continues to grow with resorts and theme parks, movies, etc. and currently has a market capitalization of $165 billion. And Walt Disney's dream continues.

The Disney culture is well respected as highly engaged, customer-centric, and loyal to the company. In our view, Walt Disney's leadership created the culture and the conditions for continued expansion of his dreams. It was Walt Disney's enduring curiosity, understanding of the need for creating respectful employees, and his hard work that enabled the ongoing success of the company. Like Walt Disney, you can have your dreams continue after you leave. But right now, making your dream happen is about focusing on the culture you help create now, one that keeps people focused on learning, and generating value for customers. You can create the social conditions for excitement and engagement, where people continuously pursue new heights through passionate curiosity.

The challenge for the leader today is to own the transformation that is sometimes uncomfortable, ultimately courageous, and shifts from one's current practices to new practices that are more in alignment with today's world. Your role is to be the change leader, not to go around talking about the need for change! The key elements of this new role include creating a way for all your team members to see the bigger picture, including how they serve their customers. Next, there is a need to develop rapid response and adaptability. Successful leaders develop employees to become better at communicating with each other to see the bigger picture and adapt. By encouraging continuous learning, individually and collectively, you can take advantage of complex adaptive systems to grow everyone's problem-solving capabilities. This is about learning how to engage your organization in an ongoing effort to identify and solve complex problems.

In essence, the new role of the leader is about creating a culture where everyone in the organization is continuously learning about how to deliver value to the customer by solving complex problems, building effective social systems, and . . . learning how to learn. This may sound like a tall order, but it may be the only way to help your company prosper in a brand-new world.

2

From a Caterpillar to a Butterfly

"Once the soul awakens, the search begins and you can never go back. From then on, you are inflamed with a special longing that will never again let you linger in the lowlands of complacency and partial fulfillment. The eternal makes you urgent. You are loath to let compromise or the threat of danger hold you back from striving toward the summit of fulfillment."

John O'Donohue, Anam Cara: A Book of Celtic Wisdom

Many of us have experienced this moment ... Suddenly, something changes inside you, something that you can't quite easily explain to others. We know this internal shift of perspective will have ongoing value for us personally and will affect the way we see the world forever. During these a-ha moments, everything is brighter, more focused, and all of a sudden easier to understand.

Some people call it the Eureka moment. Archimedes, a Greek scientist who lived from 287 BC to 212 BC is perhaps best known for his discovery of how to determine the density of an irregular shaped object. The King wanted to make sure that his crown was made of pure gold and not mixed with silver, a lower cost metal. He asked Archimedes to solve the problem. Archimedes who, as the story goes, struggled with how to calculate the density of the crown, decided to get some rest and take a bath. It was during the bath that he had a Eureka moment. (Translated from Ancient Greek, "Eureka" means "I have found it!"). As he lowered himself into the bath, he came up with a discovery of what we now call the Archimedes principle (how do you suppose it got that name?): a body immersed in a fluid is buoyed up by a force equal to the weight of the fluid displaced by the body. The story continues that he jumped out of the bath and ran through the streets, naked, yelling, "Eureka!" Today, we don't believe that this actually happened, but we still use the Eureka term to describe these special situations of a-ha moments.

Neuroscience explains that Eureka moments are accompanied by three phases of mental activity. The first phase is when you are faced with a problem and can't find a solution. Here, brain wave patterns are normal and represent the analytical processes in action. Next, during the incubation phase when you stop thinking about the problem, there is a shift in brain activity. Delta and Gamma waves get significantly reduced indicating that the normal brain functions of memory and coordinated mental activities have diminished. These changes indicate moving from normal, analytical brain functions to a new state. Then, right before the Eureka moment, Theta waves in the front of the brain increase. This is a sign that new information is being accessed and wonderful new associations are being formed, enabling you and your brain to think about a problem in a totally new light. A new insight pops into your consciousness.

The transformation that results from this moment can feel as beautiful and dramatic as watching a caterpillar become a butterfly. First, there is the a-ha moment when you know you need to shed your old skin so you can become the new you. Then, you will be tested many times, but you will persist and grow because you know you have been transformed forever.

This transformation from a caterpillar to a functioning butterfly is *not* instantaneous. After the fifth stage of molting, the basic body of a butterfly called the chrysalis emerges. Everything is in place physically, but there is still much to be done over the next 10–14 days to grow into an adult butterfly. The wings grow and become fully functioning. The antennae are formed and grow into place. The chewing mouthpiece transforms into a sucking machine for feeding on nectar from flowers . . .

The a-ha or Eureka moment that kicks everything off is usually associated with joy and excitement, but not always . . . A different kind of a-ha moment happens when we experience a personal awakening, but simultaneously go through an initial rejection and/or strong negative reaction to whatever it is that is taking place inside of us. It usually happens when, upon recognizing the need for a significant personal change, we come to realize that making this change will require us to control our habitual behaviors in order to develop new ones.

Joyful or intimidating, exhilarating or scary, every leader needs to experience an initial a-ha moment to begin to think about their role, given the new context we all live and work in. Without an a-ha moment (and all of the positive and negative feelings it brings up), there is simply no motivation for personal change. And without this motivation, we can't begin to model necessary changes for others, creating the discipline for continuous practice.

If you recall, we mentioned that we created our Transformational Leadership workshop hoping that it would give participants a chance to experience an a-ha moment. Our program created multiple opportunities for a deep reflection on personal behaviors helping participants become more self-aware of who they are and how they are seen by others. It didn't happen for all participants, but we saw many leaders experience such a-ha moments. Some leaders, after participating in the workshop, had their direct reports attend the program, many of whom came to us and asked, "What did you do to my boss?!" What we learned from them was that their leaders returned from the program with the intention to develop new skills, listen more carefully to their employees, and deploy problem-solving responsibility more effectively. With this book, we hope to inspire some a-ha moments that will spark the desire and need for a deep personal transformation.

ONE LEADER'S UNIQUE AWAKENING

Let's start with a story where a leader had a problem, a big one ... This is a true story, but we've changed names and details to keep this leader anonymous. This particular leader was somewhat aware of which path he might take in his own development, but he still needed to reach deep inside and think about how to change his own beliefs about learning, behaviors, and habits.

Tim's drive home from work was a blur. As he pulled his car into the garage, he could not recall anything about the drive. He was lost in thought. During the ride, his head was spinning, his heart was racing, and he was singularly focused on the next day's meeting at 10 A.M. with his CEO. Earlier that day Tim learned that his major project, the Automated Global Trading IT system, needed an additional $10 million to complete and that the scheduled launch would be delayed by 9 months. Tomorrow, he would share this information with the CEO. Tim was contemplating how to tell the story. What went wrong? Who was to blame? How should they reorganize? Who should they fire? Who should they hire? How will the CEO react? Would Tim still have a job tomorrow afternoon?

The project that was now in jeopardy was a big play and strategic move for this company. The latest technology for large financial institutions in business across the globe is to have software that can help maximize profit through trading across borders and currencies. This sophisticated IT system could automatically optimize those trades. Few companies were large enough to afford this system, but Tim's company had the resources to lead the industry and be the first to take advantage of the benefits of this solution. During the next day's meeting, Tim convinced the CEO of the importance of this work. He was given the money and remained the leader of the project.

Shortly after, Tim was selected to be in a small group of leaders to participate in our Transformational Leadership Program. The program engaged six senior leaders in a learn-through-experience effort that focused on effective problem-solving and practicing leader social skills to support the system problem-solving focus. One key feature of the program was to be very reflective about the influence you have on the team through your social interactions. If, for example, your interaction style with people is very dogmatic, the people will respond by doing only what you want. On the other hand, if you are completely hands-off, people will do what they think is important to them but may not do what is best for the project team.

During one session, the six leaders were asked to think about their leadership style and how it might influence the team culture. Here came Tim's big a-ha moment! He began to see himself as part of the problem with the IT project rather than looking to blame others. He realized that the way he asked questions, expecting positive responses, might have led his team to hiding some of the critical problems thus not getting them addressed. He also concluded that he needed to change his interaction with team members and expect open, honest discussion about the real problems. He knew he needed to lead the culture change. He became a butterfly, and his team members started changing, too. They rapidly became more open and honest, gradually took on more personal responsibility, and soon were able to respond faster to emergent problems to prevent big disasters.

It all wasn't as easy as it sounds, but the project stayed on track and ended with a very successful launch, on time. Tim experienced a personal a-ha moment that led to change his behaviors and helped create a more trusting development team, engaged in a proactive problem-solving process.

We have each had our own leadership awakenings followed by personal transformations. Here are our very different stories.

―――――――――

MY LEADERSHIP AWAKENING

Olga Flory

I was raised to be an achiever.

When I was at school, every time I got a grade lower than an "A," my parents told me they expected better. Simply because they believed I could do better. Their belief motivated me to try harder next time and get that desired "A."

I applied the same habit to figure skating. I took it up when I was 6 years old and skated through my senior year in high school. I remember when I began to work on the Lutz, one of the most difficult jumps in figure skating, almost every attempt ended up with a fall. I must have been making the same mistake because every time I jumped, I fell on my right hip. By the end of practice, I could barely walk. The pain was excruciating. At home, I discovered an ugly bruise on the hip area. Nevertheless, I showed up at the rink the next day and tried the Lutz again ... and again ... until two weeks later I finally landed it.

I maintained this stubborn attitude through college and made good grades. After college, I quickly landed a job and began to move up the ranks. About 10 years later, I got my first executive title, which I thought was an acknowledgment of my achievements and a confirmation of my excellent leadership abilities.

Let me add a twist! I grew up in a country (Russia) where, despite all the rhetoric about the importance of people and the value of teamwork, a top-down, command-and-control approach was a norm. A leader was the ultimate problem solver expected to get the job done and deliver results at any cost while ensuring the subordination and compliance of his or her people. Even after the collapse of the Soviet Union, despite the country's attempts to shift to a new economic and political model, the autocratic leadership model remained prevalent.

I see now that my leadership style and preferences got shaped under the influence of two factors: my deeply ingrained belief that I needed to achieve the goals I set for myself no matter what, and my country's dominant leadership approach. I sincerely believed that the best way for leaders to support their teams was to provide answers to their questions in order to "help people do a good job." In my personal development, I focused on building capabilities such as setting goals and organizing people to achieve them, making decisions under pressure, developing an effective communication style, which primarily meant being succinct and clear in my instructions, etc.

It wasn't until I was promoted to the role of Deputy General Manager at a Coca-Cola HBC plant in western Russia that I began to question this style of leadership. The person who influenced the shift in my thinking was the plant's General Manager Silviu Popovici.

On my first day in the new role, after I arranged my stuff in a spacious new office, I decided to go see Silviu so we could talk about the plan for the day. But when I got to his office, he wasn't there. His assistant explained that Silviu was on his daily walk around the plant. She said he went through the same routine every morning, starting in the Production area, then stopping at the Lab, checking on Maintenance, then proceeding to the Warehouse and completing the walk in the Sales department. She checked her watch and told me that at this time, I should be able to find Silviu at the warehouse.

Indeed, I did. I found Silviu talking to the warehouse supervisor about the problems the night shift ran into when loading trucks for cross-docking deliveries. From time to time, he would ask a question, listen to the answer, then ask another question. It was clear he wasn't there to blame the supervisor or "catch" anyone in a wrongdoing. He was simply seeking to understand what happened, wanting to know what worked and what didn't. As I listened to the supervisor, I started forming possible solutions to problems in my head curious to hear what Silviu's solution would be. To my surprise, he didn't offer any. Instead he asked the supervisor what *he* planned to do, listened to the answer, asked a few more questions, then nodded and asked to be kept informed of progress.

As we walked out of the warehouse, I asked Silviu why he didn't offer any ideas of his own. Surely, he had some! "I might have," he said. "But since I don't know every aspect of the work at the warehouse as well as this guy does, why would I volunteer solutions? I just wanted to make sure he had all the information he needed to work on the problem and that he knew I was there to support him."

This conversation put a crack in my beliefs about leadership. As I started accompanying Silviu on these walks, I listened intently to every conversation, registering his questions in my mind and watching people's reactions. I liked what I saw and quickly attempted to replicate Silviu's approach.

I didn't change overnight. There were ups and downs as I attempted to transform from a knower to a learner. After a few weeks in my new role, Silviu asked me to look into the problems with cross-docking deliveries. I diligently reviewed all available reports and came to him on the very next day with a couple of solutions. He listened, thanked me for my analysis, and then asked if I happened to see what was going on in the warehouse during the night shift (when trucks from distribution centers came to the plant to pick up next-day orders). He explained that while reports provided a lot of valuable information, it would be good to actually observe the situation first-hand, talk to the drivers and warehouse workers, and hear what *they* thought about the problems.

I followed Silviu's advice and spent several nights at the warehouse. Then I made a couple of truck rides to and from distribution centers to better understand why the drivers couldn't stay on schedule. It didn't take long to figure out why all my great solutions wouldn't solve the problems we were facing. This would ordinarily be a blow to my self-esteem, but instead, I was excited to see people opening up. Folks were eager to share their experiences with me and make suggestions. I continued building relationships that eventually helped all of us solve the problem. My personal "prize" came in the shape of a flower bouquet that truck drivers handed me at the company New Year's party as a thank you for working with them to resolve the problem.

Later, when I relocated to the U.S. and joined the Lean Enterprise Institute, I met many people who contributed to my further development as a leader. They helped me to identify the habits I needed to change to become the type of leader I wanted to be: a leader who is not afraid to show vulnerability and admit that he/she doesn't know everything, a leader who realizes that while results are important, it is the *means* for achieving them that truly matter, a leader who understands that being a hero with solutions for every problem is ineffective in today's world where interdependence and reliance on others are critical for the success of any undertaking.

I feel blessed to have been given an opportunity to re-think my view on leadership and have been thoroughly enjoying every moment of my personal transformation journey, which, as I know now, is never going to end.

MY LEADERSHIP AWAKENING

Jim Luckman

I had my first awakening and call to action in the early 1990s when I attended an accelerated 6-week leadership development program at the University of Pittsburgh. At the time, I was a Chief Engineer of Ignition Systems for Delco, Remy, responsible for the product development of these systems for General Motors. The program was designed for leaders from all industries and we had a diverse group from all over the world. There were about 20 of us learning together, and the course felt like the equivalent to a mini MBA program. We learned strategy, economics, leadership, statistics, and financial tools. For me, the most impactful day was when Clyde walked into the classroom.

Clyde was a rugged looking character who spoke with a booming, commanding voice, and addressed us with no notes, no slides, and no props. He simply stood in front of us and told his personal story about creating a remarkable change as the plant manager in an aluminum processing plant in Cleveland Ohio. He had been asked to move to Cleveland from the West Coast to be the manager of the plant that had the worst performance of all the plants in the corporation. This manufacturing plant was filled with disgruntled operators, a militant union, and supervision with little energy to address problems. As he walked into the facility, he noticed broken windows, people walking throughout the plant instead of being at their workstations, broken down equipment, general disarray, and loud arguments between union representatives and supervisors.

Clyde did not follow the typical approach for plant managers in his company. He spent a full month walking around, talking to the people, and listening to complaints. He continued doing this until he was able to interact with every single person in that plant. When Clyde had completed his analysis of the problem situation, he made some simple changes. He created "Clyde's List," a list of problems identified by the people on the floor. He then began to fix each of the legitimate problems, one at a time. He addressed the problems that were not legitimate by taking time to personally discuss the situation with the requester. He looked for alternatives and developed mutual agreements on next steps. Then he began to address some policies and procedures that seemed to be causing systemic problems.

Within nine months after Clyde's arrival, the people working in the plant shut down the union. Peace was re-established, and control was in the hands of the newly energized workforce. The following year, the performance of this plant moved from last place within the company to first place, a remarkable change given the short timeframe.

Clyde's story triggered an a-ha moment for me. Would I ever be able to make a culture change like Clyde? Unfortunately, I did not understand at the time that I could begin immediately at transforming the culture in my current job as Chief Engineer. My a-ha moment may have been inspired by Clyde's story, but I waited to test myself and attempt my own transformation as a leader later on, when I had my next job change. When I started the new gig, I had another awakening moment that changed me forever. I got connected to my greater purpose. From then on, I became more curious about everything and developed a deeper passion for continuous learning.

I see now that I actually had the opportunity three different times in my career to lead a culture change to create a new culture of problem solvers.

My first experience truly leading differently happened in 1996, five years after meeting Clyde. I finally accepted my first call to action when I was assigned a new role as plant manager. Prior to this point, my whole career was in product development leaving me completely unprepared for the new manufacturing job. The union, the people, and the business situation were all significant challenges. I wanted to make a Clyde-like change. I engaged some of the departments in 5S activities that led to performance levels well above the rest of the plant. But, although there was improvement, I did not achieve success like Clyde. After 14 months, I was assigned to a new role, the Chief Engineer and Site Manager at a technical center in Rochester, New York. I returned to my product development roots.

My second experience in leading differently happened when I moved back into engineering taking my desire to make a change to my new assignment. What I learned as plant manager about Lean and the Toyota Management System, I experimented with at the R&D center. I began by engaging a lab technician with 5S and value-stream mapping, essential Lean tools. These efforts took on a life of their own, growing across other labs and into other functions. I then enlisted help from Al Ward who studied Lean Product Development at Toyota. He had us experiment with new ways of team-oriented product development. We saw significant improvements in lead-time and quality of these projects. Technical Center Rochester became a Lean Product Development showcase. During this time, 3½ years, we hosted hundreds of benchmarking visits with people who wanted to see Lean implementation in R&D. The technical center was operating at significantly new performance levels and the employee satisfaction surveys were at the highest levels ever.

My third transformation opportunity was when I became the CEO of a small start-up company. In this facility, I used the same engagement models as before and the results were again performance improvements and employee enthusiasm. This time we reached the tipping point in about four months, a much faster pace than before.

Each of these engagements was a new phase of learning for me. I learned more about culture transformation and my role as a leader each time. And then in 2001, I decided to totally change my career. For the last 18 years, I have worked as a coach and consultant with large and small companies across diverse industries including finance, healthcare, pharmaceuticals, materials science research and development, government, consumer goods, universities, and automotive companies. Through this work, my learning has continued. Across all industries, the problems are fundamentally the same because the foundational operational assumptions are the same. I find myself on a continuous learning journey that's really all about understanding how to help leaders transform their organizations.

AWAKENINGS CONNECT US TO A MORE AUTHENTIC SELF

There comes a time when we are driven to leave our ordinary world behind and venture into the unknown. There is a surrender that takes place where you let go of your former self. All your ambitions, beliefs, and dreams—the very definition of who you are supposed to be—are stripped away. This is all replaced with a clear vision of your larger purpose, something that transcends boundaries. Something that moves and inspires you (and inspires others) because you begin transmitting energy from the *real* you, the one that knows your real purpose in life.

Joseph Campbell, an American Mythologist who defined the steps of the Hero's Journey, describes the signs that you might be in an awakening if:

- You realize you are not avoiding responsibility, but instead, you just know the journey is dramatically different and you take different actions.
- When you listen to your calling, it is familiar but frightening. You will need to balance between these two and be prepared that your judgment can impair your vision of the future.
- You feel you have reached the end of your current journey. You now feel empty about what used to make you happy.
- Your calling found you and it was unexpected.

Your unique understanding of the new role of the leader in today's world and your a-ha moment may not happen at the same time. We just hope that this book inspires you to make a personal change, take action, and experiment ... even if it takes a while as it takes a caterpillar to become a butterfly. We want to help you think about who you are as a leader because we know the benefit of taking the time to do this. The first step for you is to become more aware of your current situation and understand some simple, but powerful concepts that can help you lead more effectively.

Part 2

Awareness

For learning to be effective, the personal a-ha moment functions as a call to action. This is the moment of recognition that what one presently knows may not be enough to create meaningful change, let alone a total paradigm shift that one may not even know is necessary. This moment is a catalyst that sparks the desire to learn and ignites the learning.

In this section, we introduce three concepts that, we believe, are critical for being an effective leader in the 21st century. They directly impact your ability to lead your organization's change process from its current state to a much more effective future state.

First, we talk about the complexity of the world we live in, how "*complex adaptive systems*" work, and the need for you as a leader to be mindful of both as you try to figure out how to best support your team. Then, we introduce two paradigms that inevitably influence leadership thinking and behaviors. We discuss the effects of these on your team's agility and effectiveness at solving problems in complex adaptive systems.

Lastly, we examine unquestioned assumptions that lay at the foundation of these two contrasting paradigms. Our goal in this chapter is to help you learn to identify which assumptions happened to have shaped you as a leader so that you can see the impacts of your personal assumptions on your organization.

3

Complex Adaptive Systems

"Often, scholars distinguish between complex systems—systems in which the entities follow fixed rules—and complex adaptive systems—systems in which the entities adapt. If the entities adapt, then the system has a greater capacity to respond to changes in the environment."
Scott E. Page, Diversity and Complexity

Every organization is a complex adaptive system. Changing its culture requires an understanding of how complex adaptive systems work.

Unfortunately, most change approaches are top-down and managed by a "change manager." But we know by now that these approaches are largely unsuccessful. This is because culture change starts at the bottom and simply cannot be managed from above. Culture change grows from within the system as a result of interactions between people. With so many individual players, moving parts, and dynamics going on in any one system, this makes for an extraordinary amount of complexity.

SO WHAT ARE COMPLEX ADAPTIVE SYSTEMS ANYWAY?

The world is filled with examples of complex adaptive systems. Our environment has many interdependent parts working together, including human influences, to create a unique ecosystem. A fetus evolves from a cell to a complex organism, each cell having the intelligence of its own as it becomes a part of the liver, lungs, brain, or the eyes of the fetus. Our brains are composed of synapses that emerge to create memories and actions, which then help us make decisions. The ups and downs of the stock market are a result of many daily interactions between buyers and sellers. Business markets *emerge* (we'll talk about *emergence* soon) and grow out of the individual interactions of competitors and customers who make often unpredictable choices. And, finally, organizational behaviors, systems, processes, and outcomes are a result of how individuals and teams work together at solving problems (or not solving problems!) every day and over time. That's a lot of complexity.

Still, knowing this, we tend to think of systems in terms of linear relationships between inputs and outputs. Even the best leaders do this. For example, if we hire 10% more resources, we expect to have a 10% improvement in throughput. But complex adaptive systems are *nonlinear*: a small change to a team can result in performance improvements beyond our imagination, or we may see no impact whatsoever. This nonlinearity comes from many feedback loops, both positive and negative. Positive feedback produces exponential growth while negative feedback returns the system to the normal state.

What is one of the most critical features of a complex adaptive system? You guessed it … its ability to *adapt*. If a change occurs, individuals in the system interact, self-organize, and provide the most optimal response to the situation. Sometimes, a small change can create massive changes in system outcomes. This is known as the butterfly effect as described by Edward Lorenz in explaining the exponential nature of weather causing tornados. A flapping of a butterfly's wings in South America can affect the weather in Texas. Yes, we are talking about butterflies again!

Emergence is another core property of a complex adaptive system. In short, you might think of this simply as "the sum being greater than the parts." Individuals, interacting with each other, produce outcomes that are not guided by goals or strategies, but instead are the results of the system adapting to external situations. An example of emergence is when one group starts to benefit from applying new tools and concepts, and other groups, recognizing the benefits, quickly begin to adopt these tools and concepts without any directives from leaders. Emergence can be a very good thing, not just a symptom of the unpredictability of the world and of human beings.

HOW TO RECOGNIZE COMPLEX ADAPTIVE SYSTEMS

Remodeling a House—Example 1

After months of walking through open houses and drooling over pictures in *House Beautiful* Magazine, Sarah and John finally agreed on the approach to remodeling their house. They decided to upgrade the kitchen and expand their family room, which would require tearing down a wall and making some structural changes.

It took several months of regular meetings with a well-respected architect to agree on the final design. Then, through careful evaluation and analysis, they selected a general contractor, the person to manage the project, and they were now prepared to move on to the construction phase.

The general contractor laid out a plan and followed it, step by step, to complete the building process. They poured the concrete foundation, framed the structure, installed floors, built walls and an extension of the roof, embedded plumbing and wiring, added insulation and wallboard, installed cabinets, and finished the interior with trim, paint, and flooring. The last step was to have a final walk through, create a punch list for minor corrections, and then hand it all to Sarah and John to enjoy the newly renovated rooms.

The general contractor worked with specialists and sub-contractors specifying job requirements and making sure the work was performed in an orderly sequence. Each subcontractor working on the project was expected to inspect the quality of their work before they handed it off to the next crew. In short, the management of this project was a typical top-down, command and control process. It was executed under the assumption that all contributors were functioning as independent parts and could be controlled through direct orders.

Remodeling a House—Example 2

A large and complex structure has provided safety and comfort to its residents for many years. And then something horrible happened: a severe rain storm ripped off a major part of the structure, leaving a large gaping hole, which exposed one side to the outside world. For the first few minutes after the horrific event, the inhabitants frantically ran around in panic, not knowing what to do. Then one of them started digging in an area near the breach and created a dirt ball. Soon the erratic movements of inhabitants began to slow down, and many of them began digging, creating more dirt balls, and placing them near the breach. In the next few minutes, yet more inhabitants began to copy these actions. They started to use dirt balls to form walls, new chambers, chimneys, and tunnels. After several hours of work, the hole in the external wall was completely repaired, and the new internal structures began to take form! The rebuilt parts looked different but performed just as well as the original structure. Temperature control was restored, and the tunnels were ready for the home dwellers to move and carry food inside the habitat. All was functioning well, maybe even better.

You may have guessed by now that this structure was a termite mound. At nearly 20 feet high and 90 feet in diameter at the base, this mound served as the home for two million termites named Macroterms, and was one of the many mounds covering the deserts of Namibia, Africa. Termite mounds are built to withstand significant daily temperature swings. Inside the mound, the queen's chamber and fungus farm are located below ground, deep inside the structure, where the temperature is controlled to ±2 degrees Fahrenheit with external daily temperature swings from freezing to 75 degrees F. The termites' "home" is powered by solar energy. The surface heat from the sun creates air flows inside the mound to regulate temperature and provide ventilation. The way the mound is built supports an exchange of gases between carbon dioxide and oxygen, so in essence, it functions just like a human lung. What is truly remarkable is the fact that these incredible structures are the result of *millions of actions performed without a leader ... and with no instructions.*

These two remodeling stories clearly show the difference between a complex, or rather complicated system, and a "complex adaptive system." Sarah and John's remodeling is based on the assumption that all parts are relatively independent. Each subcontractor is responsible for getting a part of the job done, and all the parts come together under the management of the leader. This type of a system needs someone giving orders who attempts to create a logical way of engaging each part of the system at the right time (a schedule).

In comparison, over at the termite mound, there is nobody to give orders and everything is still ok. The parts interact with each other and adapt *together.* What emerges as a result of the workings of this complex adaptive system is a repaired structure that is able to weather the storms of the future.

In simplest terms, you might think of it this way:

A **complicated system** has a leader and is *controllable and predictable*, whereas a **complex adaptive system** is *leaderless, self-organizing, and adaptable* and the **outcome** is *emergent* and not *predictable*. This does not imply that culture change happens without a leader, it needs leadership that will become apparent in Part 3, Action.

A QUICK DETOUR INTO THE HISTORY OF (THINKING ABOUT) COMPLEX ADAPTIVE SYSTEMS

In 1687, Isaac Newton wrote a book, *Mathematical Principles of Natural Philosophy*, that rocked the world with ideas and principles of mechanical motion that we still use today. The concepts in the book described a world as predictable, stable, repeatable, controllable, and supported by mathematics. From that moment on, for over 200 years, the world was guided by the laws of Newtonian physics.

It wasn't until 1900 that this stable and predictable worldview was challenged by Max Planck who presented an alternate theory called Quantum Physics. He was studying energy and matter and concluded that some characteristics could not be understood inside the Newton's paradigm. Then, just a few years later, in 1905, Albert Einstein published four papers on space, time, mass, and energy that supported Plank's theories, contributing to Modern Physics' understanding of the uncertainty of the world.

Despite Planck's and Einstein's discoveries, until mid-1900s, most scientists still believed that the world is nothing else but the sum of its parts, and that in order to understand the system, they needed to break it down into individual parts and study each part individually. This approach was called *reductionist thinking*. As the world was becoming increasingly complex, however, some scientists began to work on a different approach to understanding and solving problems, which got labeled *systems thinking*. These scientists looked at how individual parts interacted with each other and, through working together, enhanced the performance of the system.

Alongside physicists, biologists attempted to understand the organic world and how plants, animals, and humans evolved to our current state. All these efforts led to a greater understanding of systems and, by the mid-1980s, a think-tank called the Santa Fe Institute in New Mexico was formed to further understand complexity. They assembled an interdisciplinary team of specialists from economics, physics, biology, ecology, and archaeology, which created the concept of the *complex adaptive system*.

Today, scientists agree that much of our world lives in complex adaptive systems, which, as we concluded earlier, are neither predictable, nor controllable, with system characteristics emerging from the interactions of individual parts. But unfortunately, most business leaders still operate under the principles created by Newton. There's a learning gap between science and business.

WHAT DOES LEADERSHIP IN COMPLEX ADAPTIVE SYSTEMS LOOK LIKE?

A dominant paradigm in most organizations is based on the assumptions of complicated systems, not complex adaptive systems. Traditional leaders believe they are responsible for controlling the system through metrics, KPIs (Key Performance Indicators), and regular reviews.

Again, a complex adaptive system is essentially leaderless. Any individual in the system can naturally assume a leadership position and be replaced by another individual at any time. But this absolutely does not mean leadership is lacking altogether. Without leadership, organizations would be overcome by chaos. A flock of geese, for example, has a rotation of leaders in the leader position. This position is more strenuous than other positions in the V formation, which is why individual birds take turns leading. In the workplace, where people are working in problem-solving teams inside complex adaptive systems, the leader's position can be self-selected and accepted by the group. The system is self-organizing.

The first task for modern leaders who understand that their companies are complex adaptive systems and cannot be controlled by giving orders is to build a framework for teams of people who want to work together toward a common purpose. We call it the *Framework for Problem Solving*. Using this framework, you can initiate, support, and create the conditions for a cultural transformation in your organization.

Described further in Chapter 6, the purpose of organizations with the framework for problem solving is to deliver value to the end customer. While most companies are structured by functions, the leader needs to design and initiate experiments for bringing together people from different functions to solve problems of value-creating processes that bridge cross-functional boundaries to serve the customer.

The next step is to provide a newly formed team with the tools and processes for system problem-solving. The leader models a communication style that is characterized by openness and transparency and encourages every individual to share their perspective of the problem situation. The leader's role is to create the environment for open dialogue so that trust and respect can grow.

Finally, the leader needs to reinforce learning through a disciplined process of deep structured reflection to help the team solve customer delivery problems by adopting the core characteristics of a complex adaptive system. Reflecting with the team, the leader designs and assesses countermeasures to support growth and continued problem-solving effort. The leader may then select a new team to evolve into the complex adaptive system in another part of the company. In the third part of the book, Action, we provide more detail on how leaders can develop a culture that intentionally embraces and grows the characteristics of complex adaptive systems in order to solve problems within larger complex adaptive systems.

As a leader, are you prepared to accept the idea that your organization is so complex that it cannot be controlled single-handedly by you? That your job is not to solve problems on your own but to create an environment for effective problem solving in service of creating value for customers?

If so, keep reading!

4

Two Paradigms

"You are free to create your own paradigms instead of simply accepting those presented to you by others."

Russell Eric Dobda

So far we've agreed that complex adaptive systems exist everywhere, and that leaders need new skills to work with these systems, especially when they attempt to take their organization on a change journey. Now we want to talk about two paradigms that, we believe, influence how we think and act, individually and collectively, when change is introduced: *the paradigm of Imposing Blanket Solutions* and *the paradigm of Problem Solving for Complexity*. Wrapping your head around these two paradigms will make it easier to change the way you lead.

> Paradigm means a pattern or a model, a generally accepted perspective, a particular way of looking at or thinking about something, which is based on a set of common assumptions. Paradigms influence our judgment and hinder the ability to understand what is going on inside a paradigm that is different from ours.

But first, a story.

Banks lend money to people who have assets for collateral. It is a modus operandi of the banking industry, right? Or, rather, it had been until one brave person challenged this long-standing banking rule.

In the mid-1970s, Mohammad Yunus, at that time a professor of economics in the University of Chittagong in Bangladesh, took a group of students on a field trip to the village of Jobra located in a poor rural area of the country. Watching people working hard yet unable to make ends meet made a profound impression on Yunus, and he began thinking about ways to help. Fired up by his belief that everybody is a natural entrepreneur, he started by giving a small personal loan to a group of female basket weavers, an action that banks would never consider.

Yunus watched these women take the investment, carefully purchase basic materials, and grow their business. Within a short time, his loan was repaid. He tried it again with another group of basket weavers in the same village. Again, he quickly recovered his investment. Then he tested the concept in a different village and saw the same positive results.

With one success after another, Yunus built a micro-lending business and in 1983 formed the Grameen Bank, meaning "village bank," founded on principles of accountability, mutual trust, creativity, and participation. Today, Grameen has over 2,500 branches that serve 8.3 million borrowers in over 80,000 villages in Bangladesh. Grameen methods have spread across 58 countries, including the U.S., Canada, France, the Netherlands, and Norway.

Now, we are learning about the limitations of the Grameen Bank model. For example, as journalist Katherine Moeller reported in her 2019 New Yorker article, "The Ghost Statistic that Haunts Women's Empowerment," scholars Ananya Roy and Lamia Karim have demonstrated that microfinance models like Grameen Bank' model can also have adverse effects on the women they intend to serve, including increased debt and domestic violence. These findings are yet another illustration of the unpredictability of complex adaptive systems and our inability to control every possible outcome. Even with all the good that came from Grameen, there were unanticipated consequences.

Despite these findings, we think Grameen Bank is still a good example of social enterprise (and trust in the human spirit). This story is also a remarkable illustration of the successful transformation of a dominant paradigm. It will continue to be if Grameen Bank addresses the unanticipated consequences of its own model.

Basic assumptions underlying business paradigms get challenged fairly often. But complete paradigm shifts like this are rare because they require change to take place at several levels. Assumptions drive our thinking, our thinking results in behaviors, and our behaviors translate into company policies and procedures. Transforming your existing paradigm into something entirely different requires a complete organizational makeover, which usually includes a personal makeover, too. Neither is easy. But, as the saying goes, a journey of a thousand miles begins with a single step. When it comes to paradigm transformation, step one is about creating awareness of the current paradigm you work and live in and then developing a vision for a future-state paradigm that helps you challenge long-accepted, deeply entrenched behaviors and habits.

TWO CONTRASTING LEADERSHIP PARADIGMS: IMPOSING BLANKET SOLUTIONS & PROBLEM SOLVING FOR COMPLEXITY

The paradigm of Imposing Blanket Solutions refers to quick solutions that companies apply, often repeatedly, not always taking the time to understand the complex nature and multi-dimensional scope of problems. No wonder these solutions rarely work: they are designed to eliminate the symptoms of problems, not their root causes. And if causes are left intact, the problems will inevitably re-occur. In contrast, the paradigm of Problem Solving for Complexity supports our ability to make weighed, intentional decisions based on a thorough analysis of facts and data, test countermeasures through rapid experimentation to allow for unpredictability, and develop solutions that will address causality and thus improve overall performance.

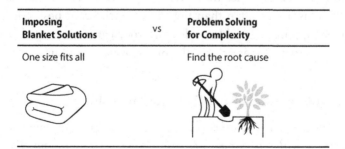

FIGURE 4.1
Two Contrasting Leadership Paradigms.

HOW TO KNOW WHEN YOU'RE IN THE PARADIGM OF IMPOSING BLANKET SOLUTIONS

Leaders who operate inside the Imposing Blanket Solutions paradigm rarely take into consideration the complex adaptive nature of their organizations. They believe that they can control processes and single-handedly solve problems inside individual functions without considering the impacts of their actions on the overall organization and its end customer. The solutions they impose on their companies can be, on most part, grouped into three categories: Copycat Solutions, Fad Programs, and One-Size-Fits-All Solutions.

Copycat Solutions

We use this term to describe solutions that leaders attempt to use over and over after their first successful application. You may ask, why is this wrong? Why can't an effective solution be used more than once? The answer is there's nothing wrong with it ... as long as the decision to apply this particular solution is based on a thorough understanding of the problem it is supposed to address.

Unfortunately, companies with a dominant Imposing Blanket Solutions paradigm have a bias for action, always trying to generate a quick, decisive response to every problem in the shortest timeframe. This is why they usually don't take the time to dig into problems to understand causality and develop countermeasures that would target the root causes. Instead, leadership teams that operate under this paradigm prefer to resort to solutions that can be implemented quickly. And the quickest way to find a solution is to re-use ones that have already been used ... even though these solutions, more often than not, don't work or, at best help remove only the symptoms of problems, leaving root causes intact ... which of course means that sooner or later the problems will reoccur.

Copycat Solution to Solve a Distribution Problem

In late 1990s, I (Olga) worked at a bottling group of a global soft-drink manufacturer with operations in Africa, Europe, and Russia. For a long time, the company ran its supply chain using a warehouse-based delivery model, which worked quite well except for the high cost of owning or renting warehouses in distribution centers. This was why the leadership team came up with an idea to switch to a different delivery model. We called it cross docking. In this new model, daily orders from distribution centers were supposed to be e-mailed or faxed to the plant at the end of the day for the night shift to assemble and package them. Once delivery drivers in distribution centers completed their routes and returned to the base, they would hand their trucks to night drivers who would drive to the plant, get the trucks loaded with next day's orders and bring them back to the distribution center. In the morning, delivery drivers would hop in their trucks and start daily routes to deliver the product to the customers.

When this new approach was piloted in western Europe, the results showed significant cost savings while customers still enjoyed a 24-hour product delivery and the high level of customer service. Having demonstrated the success of the cross-docking system, the company decided to expand it to other markets, including Russia, where it didn't work quite as expected.

The success of the system in Europe largely depended on the ability of night drivers to run on a tight schedule, allowing plant warehouses to take care of one distribution center at a time, following a pre-planned sequence. Backups happened, but they were usually minor and didn't affect the overall schedule. Russia was a different story. Telling this story requires a quick history lesson.

In 1812, two factors significantly contributed to the fiasco of Napoleon Bonaparte's Russian campaign: the bone-chilling winter and a poor condition of Russian roads. A quote attributed to the emperor stated, "In Russia, there are no roads, only directions." Ironically, the same two factors affected the introduction of cross docking when the company decided to apply it in Russia. Night drivers struggled to execute rides from distribution centers to the plant on schedule, particularly in wintertime. Every night, trucks from at least a couple of distribution centers would arrive later than expected. As a result, they had to get to the end of the line and wait for hours to be loaded. Naturally, they would return to their distribution centers late, thus affecting the routines of day drivers, which, in turn, meant that many customers didn't get their product on time.

The company tried to make adjustments but nothing seemed to work. In the meantime, aggravated drivers and warehouse staff began to quit, unwilling to deal with the pressure of unrealistic schedules. Unhappy customers turned to competitors. After several months of futile efforts to make the system work, the company had to admit the approach failed and made a drastic change. A 24-hour delivery promise to the customer was replaced with 48 hours, which allowed building some flexibility into the system. This meant that all the contracts had to be re-signed, schedules re-calculated, market developers needed to be re-trained to learn how to forecast a 48-hour demand, and customers needed to be convinced that the new delivery schedule wouldn't affect their business. Eventually, the system began to work, but it came with a significant price tag as well as deteriorated morale, increased turnover, loss of customers, etc. What appeared to be a great solution in one case turned out to be a hassle in another. Copycat solutions are often harmful to the health of an organization, enticing as they may be at first glance.

Fad Programs

Most fad programs are driven from the top. With the best intentions, of course! The purpose of most fads is to improve work processes and, as a result, improve their outcomes to the customer, make positive changes to the organizational culture, and increase the ability of a company to attract and retain best talent.

But in reality, fad programs tend to translate into endless meetings, new buzzwords, procedures, artifacts, and a tremendous amount of extra work for frontline employees and supervisors. What is one common characteristic of fads? They always start with a bang, then slow down, and fade into oblivion, after which someone on the leadership team comes up with a *new* idea, which typically steers the company in yet another different direction.

We are not the only ones to be critical of fad programs. Geoffrey James, a writer and a contributor to CBS' MoneyWatch, put together a list of the stupidest business fads of all time. In no particular order, here are some of them:

- Six Sigma, an approach to quality management created by Motorola.
- Business Process Reengineering—used to analyze business processes and rework them to achieve a defined business outcome.
- Matrix Management—an attempt to combine direct and dotted reporting relationships.
- Management by Objectives—evaluation of employee performance against a previously agreed upon set of objectives.
- Core Competency/competencies—focusing on what a company does (wants to do) better than anybody else and identifying critical skills needed to succeed.

Note that we mention only what these fads are intended to do and stay away from describing their real impacts—it is not our goal to examine the outcomes of these fad programs. If you have lived through one or more of these, you know how devastating their impacts can be for everyone involved.

ONE-SIZE-FITS-ALL SOLUTIONS

Here we are talking about reorganizations, layoffs, outsourcing candidates for senior leadership positions, changes in naming conventions, introduction of new software, the use of social media, and, of course, an all-time favorite . . . *training*!

One-Size-Fits-All Solution—A Training Program Rollout

Not long ago, a large U.S.-based service company started a campaign to re-brand itself as "a global business." When the strategy was announced, every department began to shift business priorities, intro-duce new projects, make structural changes, adjust budgets, etc. Talent Practice group's contribution came in the form of a training program, which was supposed to demonstrate the benefits of developing the mindset of a global leader. To design and facilitate the training, they contracted a highly recommended (expensive!) vendor who was tasked to deliver the program to all 6,000 company managers within a 12-month time-frame. In addition to the vendor fees, the company would need to cover participant travel expenses and carry the cost of taking six thousand people off their jobs for a full day, so you get an idea of the price tag for this project.

The talent group came up with this idea after they learned that a few C-suite leaders who were promoted to new roles on the global leadership team had little to no experience in running international operations. They clearly needed some support in developing the perspective and habits of a global leader. Was training the right solution for them? Possibly, although, obviously, not the only one. What is hugely unclear is how this training would be useful for a mid-level manager based, say, in the U.S. Midwest who served local customers only and had no exposure to global operations.

But … one size fits all, and the decision had been made. Later we learned that, to the credit of the company executive team, upon reviewing the proposed budget and expected deliverables, they asked the Talent group to reconsider this initiative and focus on helping just those leaders whose jobs were affected by the globalization of the company business.

HOW TO KNOW WHEN YOU'RE IN THE PARADIGM OF PROBLEM SOLVING FOR COMPLEXITY

When you walk into an organization that has made progress in building the practice of problem-solving, you can see and feel the difference. You see people from different departments and functions working collaboratively at identifying and solving delivery problems. You see energized, engaged, and focused teams. You observe leadership practices and behaviors that are geared toward supporting problem-solving teams. And you notice how differently management systems and tools work when they are used to help teams expose problems in real time and reward people for their problem-solving effort.

Now, what are the drivers of this type of problem solving? What factors help establish this practice and make it bloom? Lean has taught us how to get everybody engaged in addressing problems in a structured way, continuously. After years of observing and working with various companies at various stages of their Lean journeys, we were able to capture some critical conditions that need to be in place to enable leaders and teams solve problems effectively.

Problem Solving for Complex Adaptive Systems, while it still uses the basic structure of Lean problem-solving, is more challenging because it requires problem solvers to take into consideration the *fluidity and the ever-changing nature of all processes* taking place inside an organization and be ready to respond to unpredictable, unexpected situations that constantly arise in the fast-changing world around them.

Which is why, we formulated these conditions for effective problem-solving with complex adaptive systems in mind:

Problem Solving for Complexity Recognizes the Challenges and Uses the Power of Complex Adaptive Systems

The process of Problem Solving for Complexity is *highly collaborative* in nature. No matter how knowledgeable and experienced leaders are, they value both the diversity of individual talents, perspectives and skills, and the collective wisdom of their teams. Looking at complex problems from multiple perspectives is key to not only defining a good problem but also exploring multiple solutions and selecting the best one.

Rapid learning cycles are critical for responding to feedback loops and adapting to fast-changing situations. Complex adaptive systems move as a result of the individuals' response to feedback loops, positive and negative. It is important to structure the teams in a way that helps provide feedback and respond to these signals.

Teams solving problems in complex adaptive systems need to be able to *self-organize* to meet the demands of changing needs and/or new requirements, knowing there's absolutely no way to predict what they are and when they happen. They embrace Eisenhower's "Plans are nothing; planning is everything" motto.

A structured problem-solving process for complex adaptive systems needs to *look beyond root causes* and examine the interdependencies of the system. Unlike linear transactional processes where the variables are held constant, complex adaptive systems will not stand still. Problem solvers need to keep in mind that multiple variables not only affect each other, but they themselves may change in the process. Looking at the interactions between the parts is an important part of problem solving for complexity.

Problem Solving for Complexity is grounded in the scientific method of PDCA, or the Plan, Do, Check, and Adjust cycle.

PDCA is based on the method of scientific experimentation that scientists have been using for hundreds, if not thousands, of years. The first known reference to this method belongs to Francis Bacon, an English statesman, philosopher, and scientist. In his book Novum Organum published in 1620, he described a cycle that is initiated by the identification of a problem to be solved and the development of a hypothesis around a possible solution. The steps in the cycle include a plan for an experiment that will help prove (or disprove) the hypothesis ("PLAN"), the execution of the experiment ("DO"), reflection on the results and the learning that came out of the experiment ("CHECK"), and then, if the experiment confirmed the hypothesis, development of a permanent solution. Or, if more proof is required, figuring out what needs to be changed ("ADJUST") and repeating the cycle.

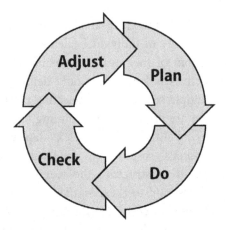

FIGURE 4.2
Scientific Method: The Plan–Do–Check–Adjust Cycle.

William Edwards Deming, an American professor, engineer, and consultant known for his work on the concepts of quality management and continuous improvement, is often given credit for introducing PDCA to the business world as a framework for effective problem-solving. We'll talk more about PDCA later, when we get to reviewing leadership *actions* that enable a transition from Blanket Solutions to Problem Solving for Complex Adaptive Systems.

Problem Solving for Complexity is Fact-Based and Supported by Data

We often use these two terms, "facts" and "data," interchangeably, although they are quite different. A quick check with Wikipedia shows that a FACT is "a statement that is consistent with reality or can be proven with evidence. The usual test for a statement of fact is verifiability." DATA is defined as "a set of values of qualitative or quantitative variables" and it usually comes in the form of graphs, images, or other analysis tools. It can be collected, measured, reported, and analyzed. It can also be interpreted or misinterpreted.

The reason for data misinterpretation can vary: incomplete information, questionable research practices, poor visualization of information, deliberate falsification and, of course, subjectivity of data recipients. We all have attended meetings where different people drew different conclusions from the same set of data and had lengthy debates defending their individual perception. Facts, on the other hand, are free from subjectivity: it is hard to question what we can see, touch, hold, smell, and/or hear. Which is why rule number one for Problem Solving for Complexity is to *start with facts that help understand the problem, then use data to substantiate the facts.*

Problem Solving for Complexity Requires Discipline and Structure, Both of Which Need to Be Introduced and Modeled by Leaders

Besides role modeling, leaders need to introduce and build into their management system the *tools, systems, and practices* that support the ability of employees to identify problems and solve them at the root cause. What it does is turn every problem-solving effort into a learning experience that can be shared with the rest of the organization so that others can benefit from it. This creates the conditions for the kind of *emergence* we spoke about earlier, where one team picks up the learning from another team. It is important as well not to force the use of tools, systems, and practices, onto the organization but help them emerge organically. Otherwise, there's a risk they will also turn into fads.

WHY BLANKET SOLUTIONS ARE STILL SO COMPELLING

For a long time, we tried to understand the causes of the insatiable appetite for quick solutions but were unable to come up with a good explanation of this phenomenon. This was until discoveries in neuroscience in the first decade of this century provided an insight into how our brain works when we learn and solve problems, make decisions, and develop skills. They helped us better understand why we rely on blanket solutions the way we do and why we struggle to develop discipline around deliberate, structured, fact-based problem-solving, which, we know to be effective for working in complex adaptive systems.

In 2011, Nobel Prize laureate Daniel Kahneman published *Thinking Fast and Slow*, where he drew a distinction between two thought modes that co-exist in a human brain: "System One" and "System Two." According to Kahneman, System One is responsible for producing *fast, instinctive, emotionally charged* solutions. When we rely on System One, we simply react to what is in front of us without looking for additional facts and/or data. "System Two" is *slower, more deliberative, and more logical*. It is responsible for structured, rational, value-based judgments. You would think that the obvious benefits of System Two should make it an automatic winner, and we (logical and rational Homo sapiens!) would rely on it to support our problem-solving and decision-making. The reality, however, is that when humans are presented with several optional approaches to problem resolution, we instinctively try to choose the one that requires the least effort.

To understand why, we need to know how our brain processes information. Every time we receive a new bit of information (verbal or non-verbal), one of 100 billion or so neurons connects with another neuron to form a new circuit. Once a new circuit is established, the brain compares it to existing connections. If it finds one that has some semblance to the new circuit, it connects the two. By the same token, when we face a problem, the first thing our brain does is look for patterns. And if it finds a previously applied solution to what looks like a similar problem, System One delivers it to us.

To us, Kahneman's book was a breath of fresh air. It helped explain what we have each observed in our engagements with many different companies. With the help of Kahneman's research and helpful framing, we solved the enigma of leadership reliance on blanket solutions, despite the obvious imperfections of this approach. *Thinking Fast and Slow* helped connect observable outcomes of pre-conceived blanket solutions with the workings of a human brain. It is our reliance on System One that makes us want to jump to quick solutions and, should they produce some visibility of problem resolution, re-use them again and again while "lazy" System Two essentially hibernates.

Sigh. Now that we know this, we can make a choice not to let System One rule our actions.

MAKING THE SHIFT: SOLVE ONE PROBLEM AT A TIME

"Forward movement is not helpful if what is needed is a change of direction."

David Fleming

In the Introduction, we mentioned that, according to several independent studies, about 2/3 of all large-scale change initiatives (read "attempts to transform their dominant paradigms") don't deliver expected outcomes. We believe that the primary reason behind these sad statistics is that most transformation approaches use their organization's existing paradigm to make a big change. Our perspective is different. We believe leaders need to take companies through change using the thinking of the new paradigm, first creating awareness of the current habits of solutions thinking and then developing new habits for problem solving for complexity.

Over time, every company develops a dominant paradigm, which is shaped by unquestioned assumptions of its leaders and employees. This paradigm, in turn, begins to influence other components of the culture: beliefs, values, systems, and practices. The impact of paradigms on organizational culture is particularly obvious at the time of change, when a company attempts to alter its culture. In other words, when its leadership team tries to accomplish a paradigm shift.

For a leader to undertake a transformation of this kind requires an acknowledgment of the existing paradigm and an understanding of the assumptions of the new paradigm that the team aspires to develop. Which is a hard thing to do! Michael Brune, Executive director of the Sierra Club, perhaps America's most influential environmental organization, commenting on paradigms around solar power and new energy technologies, has said, "*paradigm shifts aren't always obvious when you are in the middle of one.*" This could not be more true! Think about groups with contrasting dominant paradigms such as evolutionists and creationists, warmongers, and peaceniks, those who acknowledge global climate change and those who deny it, dog lovers and cat lovers, parents and teens ... If you can place yourself in one of these groups, you will agree that it is hard not just to accept, but comprehend the assumptions that drive the thinking and behaviors of the other group. Assumptions that form paradigms influence our judgment and hinder our ability to understand what is going on inside a paradigm that is different from ours.

As we mentioned at the beginning of this chapter, for a leader who wants to help his or her organization transition away from blanket solutions and master the art and science of problem solving for complexity, step one is to understand which paradigm currently influences the thinking, behaviors, and practices of their organization. How do you do it? Begin observing how people perform work, how they talk to each other, how they handle cross-functional projects, how they behave in meetings, and, of course, how they identify and tackle problems. Soon you will have enough evidence pointing to the paradigm that dominates your company.

Read the examples below. Which paradigm, do you think is responsible for these behaviors?

1. You hear people say: "The problem is that we need X" (substitute X with a specific solution such as "more training," "more people," "more agility," etc.).
2. You hear people state problems as gaps in business performance: "The problem is that our quality is 10% lower than the target."
3. You see leaders in the workplace, observing business processes, talking to people, and coaching them through their problem-solving effort.
4. You see leaders make decisions single-handedly based on the analysis of large amounts of data without ever going to the workplace.
5. You see employees use documents that describe their work to ensure they follow standards. These are constantly updated to capture process improvements.
6. Your company's processes are described in SOP manuals, which are kept in managers' offices and are rarely (or never) reviewed and/or updated.
7. You can name three company-wide initiatives that have generated a lot of buzz in the last few years but didn't produce any results.
8. All tools, systems, and practices used in your team have been introduced as countermeasures to specific problems.

Most likely, you have concluded that examples 1, 4, 6, and 7 point to the influence of the Imposing Blanket Solutions paradigm, while examples 2, 3, 5, and 8 are indicative of the paradigm of Problem Solving for Complexity. If your observations lead you to admit that your organization is influenced by blanket solutions, it's time to start planning how to transition your organization to the Problem Solving for Complexity paradigm.

In Part 3 (Action), we will get into much more detail on the actions that leaders need to take to accomplish a shift from Imposing Blanket

Solutions to Problem Solving for Complexity. Right now, we just want to say that perhaps the most important thing to remember is that you want to be careful not to attempt to transform your whole organization at once. Instead, we suggest starting with *one* business problem. Not ten problems! Not two or three! Just one. A problem, which, when solved, will have a sizeable and noticeable impact on the delivery of customer value by your team, and then continuing to solve one problem at a time.

In Part 3, we'll talk about why you want to engage experts in this problem-solving process. Note that by "experts," we don't mean Yellow/Green/Black Belts, quality assurance, and/or process excellence staffs, or external consultants. We mean people who are the closest to the work, who actually create customer value. Their contribution will have the most impact on the ability of the group to understand the problem situation.

We'll talk about how to create an open and trusting environment to help people feel comfortable identifying and attacking problems head on. Be there for them all the way! And we'll talk about how to build reflection into the problem-solving process to allow learning to take place.

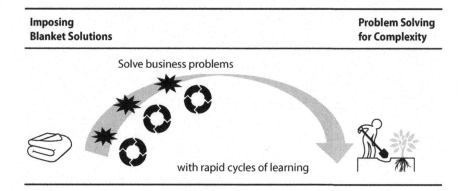

FIGURE 4.3
Organic Transformation: Solving One Problem at a Time.

By focusing on one business problem and engaging teams into the problem-solving process, you start changing the culture of your company *organically*. An organic approach to change is not project-based; you cannot draw a line at the end of the project and pronounce it done.

Nor is it tool-based, meaning we are not offering tools that were created someplace else, which may or may not be of value to your team. If you recall what we learned about complex adaptive systems, an organic approach will trigger the *emergence* of new *tools, systems, and practices* that will enable and support experimentation and learning.

For now though, let's take some time to better understand underlying assumptions beneath these two very different paradigms.

5

Unquestioned Assumptions

> "Your assumptions are your windows on the world. Scrub them off every once in a while, or the light won't come in."
>
> Isaac Asimov

As you'll learn, if you go through Gestalt training, over 90% of our actions result from unquestioned assumptions and are done without thinking at all. The remaining 10% are a result of deliberate decision-making, driven by the pre-frontal cortex. Assumptions guide our actions and make us do things without thinking, and these habitual behaviors are controlled by the area of the brain called the Basil Ganglia located deep within the hemispheres of the cerebrum. We'll say it again: leadership has a lot to do with understanding brain science.

So, if assumptions drive most of our actions, let's slow down and consider:

What are the unquestioned assumptions of your current management paradigm?

Which of these do you want to keep and embrace?

Which of these might you want to question (or may you have already started questioning)?

Let's start with a short story . . .

Peter makes his way through the front door of his neighbor Geoffrey's house after getting an urgent request from Geoffrey's wife, Sarah, asking for help because her husband was having trouble breathing. Peter has been in medical practice for 20 years and already has ideas on how to address the situation.

After greeting Sarah and listening to her describe the condition, Peter walks into the bedroom where Geoffrey is lying in bed, taking short and frequent breaths, each one a struggle. Peter reaches in his medical case and pulls out a fleam bleeder instrument and a blood bowl. He selects an

area on Geoffrey's left arm and quickly pushes a sharp blade through the
flesh until blood begins to flow into the blood bowl. When the bowl fills
about halfway, Peter puts pressure on the wound to stop the flow of blood
and then covers the area with a bandage. Over the next few days, he
returns to Geoffrey's home three more times, each time extracting more
blood. A week later, Geoffrey takes his last breath ...

This fictional account of bloodletting could have taken place at any point from antiquity to the late 19th century. Historical accounts indicate that George Washington had multiple bloodletting procedures in his final hours (1799). Some historians estimate that he had 80 ounces of blood extracted in a 12-hour timeframe. Many accounts of medical treatment during the Civil War (1861–1865) involve bloodletting. This was a popular medical practice because of the belief in Humor Theory, which indicated that there were four bodily fluids that needed to be kept in balance. If there was a symptom of illness, extracting a portion of blood from an ailing patient was supposed to work toward rebalancing the four fluids, curing the patient.

Assumptions in the efficacy of the Humor Theory simply were not questioned, and therefore bloodletting continued as a regular practice. You can see where we're going with this ...

Finally, a competing theory emerged by the late 1800s, called Germ Theory. It was supported by research and empirical evidence, pioneered by scientists like Semmelweis, Pasteur, Snow, Koch, and Lister among others. It suggested that diseases were not caused by an imbalance of bodily fluids, but rather by micro-organisms called bacteria and viruses. Since the underlying assumptions of these theories were so different, they led to different behaviors and practices by medical professionals. Doctors operating under the assumptions of Germ Theory changed the medical practices from bloodletting to the use of drugs designed to either destroy the bacteria through antibiotics or minimize the symptoms caused by viruses, leading to the significant array of medicines we see in pharmacies today.

Well, imagine that you had been practicing bloodletting for 20 years and now you are just beginning to learn about Germ Theory. How do you convince yourself that you need to move from bloodletting to a different approach? How would you lead others to move from one paradigm to the other? Just like the doctors who believed in Humor Theory needed to recognize and change their assumptions in order to accept Germ Theory, we all need to understand the assumptions of the two leadership paradigms, The paradigm of Imposed Blanket Solutions and the paradigm of Problem Solving for Complexity.

During the development of our Transformational Leadership Program, we made a list of leadership behaviors we observed across companies in a wide range of industries. Then we asked which assumptions support these behaviors and grouped them into five categories.

Let's take a look at the assumption "categories", comparing the respective assumptions of the two paradigms. The first column of Figure 5.1, shows the five assumption categories that describe the assumptions of the two different paradigms. The next two columns represent the unquestioned assumptions of the Imposing Blanket Solutions paradigm and the Problem Solving for Complexity paradigm.

In this chapter, we will cover the following:

- **Overview:** Description of the assumptions
- **Connection to Other Assumptions**: How each assumption category relates to others (if applicable)
- **Background**: A brief historical perspective and how we got here
- **Story**: An example of how people live by these assumptions
- **Limitations and Advantages:** A summary for each paradigm

		Blanket Solution Paradigm	versus	Problem Solving for Complexity Paradigm
	**Leadership Focus**	Results	vs	Means
	**Worldview**	Fragmentation	vs	System
	**Handling Change**	Command & Control	vs	Disturb & Respond
	**Social Connections**	Defensive Reasoning	vs	Internalizing
	**Creating Knowledge**	Knower	vs	Learner

FIGURE 5.1
Leadership Assumptions of the Two Paradigms.

Before you continue, a word of caution. Thinking about assumptions is hard work. It takes time to assimilate all the information and make it real. You will need to slow down and use that pre-frontal cortex for doing some deep reflection about your unique situation. There is an abundance of thought-provoking material in this chapter and we recommend you first skim through the five assumption categories by reading the titles, stop, and then think about what they might mean to you. Then go through each of the assumption pairs, one at a time. At the end of each section, we suggest that you pause and think. You can use the questions provided to help with your reflection. Reading and gathering information is different from deep reflection. Slow down and begin to build your reflection skills. This important chapter will help you understand the gaps that need to be closed to transform your own paradigm and that of your organization.

 ## LEADERSHIP FOCUS: RESULTS VERSUS MEANS

What is Most Important for Leaders to Pay Attention To?

"Just Do It." Nike's famous slogan is alive and well today, and it has been embraced by many traditional companies with one addition: "...and I will check... to *make sure* you are doing it." Deeply woven

Blanket Solution Paradigm	vs	Problem Solving for Complexity Paradigm
Results: Make profit		Means: Deliver customer value

Achieve Objectives

People

Integration

Tools   Process

FIGURE 5.2
A Comparison of Leadership Focus Assumptions.

into the culture, this focus sends a clear message to team members (not just customers!) while telling a compelling story about the values, beliefs, and assumptions of the leader. The goals, values, policies, procedures, and activities that leaders pay attention to have a profound effect on team performance. The regular meetings, action items, and e-mail messages tell a story about the fundamental assumptions of the leader and team members.

Overview

There are two basic ways to think about the assumptions that underlie leadership focus. First, where leaders focus their attention is more oriented to either the *means* (how the work is done) or the *results* (outcome of the work). There is a tendency for leaders in the Imposing Blanket Solutions paradigm to focus on the results without enough emphasis on the means by which to achieve them.

Second, leaders define purpose and then pay attention to achieving that purpose. Leaders working in the Imposing Blanket Solutions paradigm typically have objectives that are overlapping or conflicting rather than aligned to a clear purpose. Alternatively, for organizations in a Problem Solving for Complexity paradigm, leaders demonstrate clarity of purpose focused on serving value to the customer, encouraging employees to actively engage in improving the means by which to deliver value.

Background

How Did We Come to Focus so Much on Results?

The obsession with results, something deeply embedded in the Imposing Blanket Solutions paradigm, has been the practice for at least half a century. This focus on results shows up in organizational objectives at every level. In his 1954 book, *The Practice of Management*, Peter Drucker introduced the process of "Management by Objectives" with the intent to overcome the "activity trap" and create focus. Although this practice reduced some extraneous activities, the negative effect that emerged over time was an overemphasis on the results with an insufficient awareness of the means by which to meet the objectives.

Organizations with a dominant Problem Solving for Complexity paradigm focus on the means to achieve the results. John Wooden didn't "just do it." As head coach of the UCLA basketball team, he would not have been able to lead his team to win ten NCAA national championships in a period of 12 years if he didn't pay meticulous attention to the means. His practice sessions were precisely planned down to the minute. He focused on building individual capabilities and helping his team work together as a unit. He increased the pace of play for practice so that when it came to the real game, it felt like it was being played in slow motion. UCLA's results came from their relentless focus on the means by which they worked to achieve results.

In the Problem Solving for Complexity paradigm, people solve problems while doing their work, improving business processes, and running small experiments with the help of new tools, every day if possible.

How Did We Come to Believe the Purpose Is to Make Money?

Purpose has a large influence on how leaders spend their valuable time. Blanket solutions leaders tend to work with two different sets of assumptions when it comes to purpose. They either have a very large emphasis on a single purpose of maximizing profit, or they have many purposes as they are trying to provide value to stakeholders, customers, suppliers, investors, employees, etc.

The "maximize profit" assumption was described and emphasized by Milton Friedman, in a 1970 *New York Times* article, "The Social Responsibility of a Business is to Increase its Profits." Friedman, of course, was a well-respected economist at the time and a recipient of a Nobel Prize in Economics. He was promoting an efficient market model of economics based on the theory that if you make more money for your organization, you provide greater value for all involved. This idea was based on the classical liberalism model of economics. Many companies followed this model and created an emphasis on boosting their profits. Also, maximizing profit is emphasized by Wall Street through their attention to stock price for those public companies who exchange on the stock markets, making it their purpose.

Other companies have adopted a more holistic purpose of serving multiple customers. In 1984, an alternative purpose was proposed by R. Edward Freedman in his book *Strategic Management: A Stakeholder Approach*. Freedman suggested that the purpose of companies was to satisfy multiple stakeholders including management, employees, suppliers, stockholders, public, and government. This shifted leaders' thinking away from the singular profit purpose toward multiple, concurrent needs. Managing multiple objectives to serve *all* stakeholders became the standard.

Yet, each of these approaches to achieving purpose in Imposing Blanket Solutions companies still focuses on results, not the means by which people achieve results. Often, objectives (blanket solutions) are defined by senior leaders through an annual business planning process. They are then "deployed" to each function or group and individual, and then tracked throughout the year. Leaders include other blanket solution ideas in these objectives that they may want to deploy across the organization as fad programs. Nearly all activities are event oriented, with a timeline that has a clear start and end date. Leaders measure and review objectives to check on progress and assess the likelihood of their team achieving a result.

A Story about Results versus Means

"The Purpose is to Make Profit"

I (Jim) had a chance to observe the effects of the emphasis on financial results. In 1999, when the Delphi Corporation was spun off from General Motors and became its own independent company, it had its own separate stock and became a part of the financial analysis of Wall Street. The first executive meeting after the split was all about presentations and solutions on how to maximize the stock market price. Guest speakers offered ways to influence financial people who rated our stock value.

Next came a reorganization. Delphi merged the chassis division with the powertrain division, attempting to create a more positive financial image. One division was making good profit while the other one was marginal. This combination eliminated the exposure of the marginal division. Each division had a close relationship with their customers. In the end, the merger and the new organization broke the unique alignment between Delphi and their customers, either powertrain or chassis, causing confusion and complexity when it came to people actually interacting with customers.

Companies working in a Problem Solving for Complexity paradigm understand that the purpose is to deliver value to the customer. Since Delphi reorganized to a more general model, we lost valuable information about the different needs of powertrain vs. chassis.

A BRIEF REVIEW

Limitations of Overly Focusing on Results:

- Puts too much emphasis on cutting costs that can limit the performance at delivering value to customers
- The focus on financial results takes an organization's attention away from solving customer problems
- Diminishes a sense of value for employees particularly if there is an understanding of how senior leaders benefit from profit vs. lower level employees

Advantages of Focusing on the Means by Which You Achieve Results:

- Creates an important focal point for measuring performance based on the delivery of value to the customer
- Helps to define and prioritize key business problems to be solved
- Creates alignment of functions to serve the customer
- Creates a framework for distributed problem-solving
- Builds awareness and value for employees
- Enables development of employee skills

Let's pause and think together. What percentage of the effort to achieve annual goals focuses on financial performance vs. customer's needs? How much of your time is dedicated to looking for results instead of the means to achieve results (process, people, tools)? Do you have a standard problem-solving process or any problem-solving process at all? In meetings with your people, how much time is spent on getting information about the achievement of the goal or action vs. the problems with the process to achieve the goal?

 ## WORLDVIEW: FRAGMENTATION VERSUS SYSTEMS

Which Framework Do We Use to Make Sense of the World, Ourselves, and Our Lives?

The parts of the body, all the internal systems, work together to keep us alive. Let's take a look. The muscular system and the skeletal systems work together to provide movement and support. The digestive system and circulatory

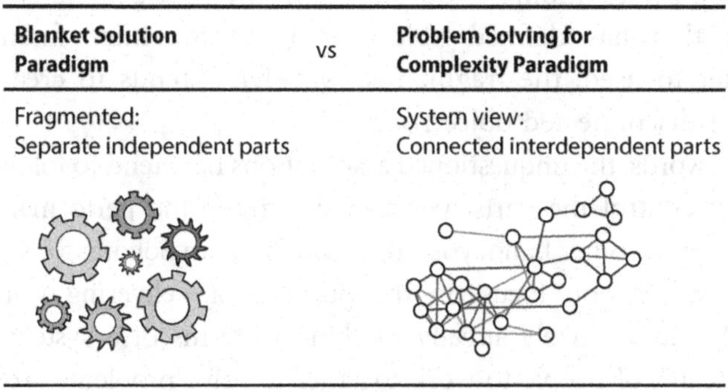

Blanket Solution Paradigm	vs	Problem Solving for Complexity Paradigm
Fragmented: Separate independent parts		System view: Connected interdependent parts

FIGURE 5.3
Comparison of Worldview Assumptions.

system work together to break down large molecules into small molecules for providing energy and deliver that energy to enter cells throughout the body. All these systems work together and are interdependent. Yet, sometimes, specialists (cardiologists, oncologists, neurologists . . .) view them as independent, each focusing on the part they specialize in, and do not consider what happens to the rest of the system.

OVERVIEW

There are some simple systems that have independent parts and can be examined by looking at each part separately. Generally, these are mechanical systems. When we're doing root cause analysis, an automotive engine, for example, in contrast to the body, can usually be analyzed as if it has completely independent parts. Problem solving for an engine, even though it is complicated, can use a simple cause-and-effect analysis to isolate the part and get to the root cause. On the other hand, diagnosing the body, with its large number of interdependencies, is a much more difficult problem.

CONNECTION TO OTHER ASSUMPTIONS

Our Worldview, the assumptions we hold to be true about the world and how we interact with it, builds on the previous set of assumptions in Leadership Attention. If you are in the Imposing Blanket Solutions paradigm that has defined objectives that are either financially or stakeholder focused, the fragmented worldview tends to create a large number of disconnected objectives.

In other words, the unquestioned assumptions here tend to follow the idea that if you control the parts, you can determine the performance of the system. If, on the other hand, you are in the Problem Solving for Complexity paradigm (when you focus on the purpose of delivering value to the customer), you are likely already thinking in terms of a system. You are engaging teams of people to work together to solve problems. You steadily improve the connections between parts, people, or functions, which will result in improving your ability to deliver value to your customer.

There are plentiful examples of companies with unquestioned assumptions based on this mechanical, reductionist model. The traditional model of the Imposing Blanket Solutions paradigm is to *fragment* an organization into functions and then *control the functions*. Then we take each function and break it down to groups and individuals. The basic theory of management is to control individuals. Personal objectives and personal performance appraisals are a normal part of the reductionist model. We tend to define problems as issues that occur as a result of a single function or person. We reorganize to create more control of some of the functions. We assume that individuals make the difference, not the way individuals interact with each other.

BACKGROUND

How Did We Get so Analytical?

The Scientific revolution, between 1550 and 1700, created a shift in thinking about reality. People went from believing that all actions were controlled by God to realizing that they could take some control by understanding that the world worked in certain ways. This shift began with Copernicus, who asserted that the sun sat at the center of the universe, that each of the planets followed a path around the sun, and that this system could be explained through a simple mechanical model. Drawing upon this discovery, Newton created a set of rules explaining the physical world, the rules that now are called Newtonian Physics.

Systems Thinking has been on an evolutionary path to move away from the simplistic mechanistic thinking of Newtonian Physics toward a better model for solving today's more difficult problems. The point here is that we need to rid ourselves of the overuse of breaking things down and attempting to control parts; it's time to move to a more effective way of viewing problems in our world through the lens of systems thinking. You'll recall how systems thinking is a foundation for working with complex adaptive systems, which we covered in detail earlier.

A Story about Fragmentation versus Systems

In 2006, I (still Jim here) facilitated a meeting with the executive committee of a large construction company. This company had many regional divisions across the United States with a wide variation in performance between them.

The purpose of my meeting with 11 executives was to introduce them to Lean Thinking and identify something they could agree on for next steps. I asked these leaders to identify their business problems. They separated into groups of three or four and created a list of problems. As they reported out their problems, I noticed they were solutions, objectives, or projects they felt a need to accomplish. They said things like, "We need better people," and "We need to reorganize" or even, "We should merge two divisions." Some people said things like, "We need a quality initiative." etc. I commented that all of these looked like solutions to a business problem and not a clear definition of a problem. I asked them to try to identify one business problem they actually have and consider how they are working to meet their customers' needs. After another 45 minutes, a different problem statement arose: "We have significant quality, timing, and profit variation from project to project."

Ok! This was a good problem statement that this team could use to create more specific projects and improve their delivery to their customers. What I then learned was that the initial problems these 11 folks listed came from a Strategic Planning offsite that had happened the previous week. A consulting firm guided them to identify an objective for each Executive, so that each one would be responsible for coming up with quick solutions. 11 objectives for 11 executives. The most disappointing part of this story is that eventually, this group chose to continue with the 11 objectives instead of working on the customer delivery variation problem. Six months after this meeting I received information that they were still attempting to correct the overlap created by the 11 objectives.

A BRIEF REVIEW

The Limiting Effects of a Fragmented Worldview:

- Puts too much emphasis on controlling the parts limiting system performance
- Puts too much emphasis on the individual reducing a team approach to problem solving
- Supports a flawed concept that things can be controlled and predictable
- Creates a sense of linear change vs. exponential growth
- Supports a model of fixing problems with a single solution

The Positive Effects of the Systems View of Interconnected Parts:

- Creates an important focal point for measuring performance based on customer value
- Helps to define and prioritize key business problems to be solved
- Creates alignment of functions to serve the customer
- Creates a framework for distributed problem-solving
- Builds awareness and value for employees
- Enables development of employee skills

Let's think together again about your mental model of the world. Do you see it as a collection of individual parts? Do you think that there is a simple cause-effect relationship? Do you think that your organizational performance is determined by a few good people? Is your company structured in separate, disconnected functions? Is each function working on their own goals that were not considered together as a system? Or, are you building teams that can solve problems together? Is your compensation system tied to individual performance or team engagement?

 ## HOW CHANGE HAPPENS: COMMAND AND CONTROL VERSUS SELF-ORGANIZATION AND EMERGENCE

What is the Best Way to Approach Change?

Does the term *"change program"* bother you? Rolling out programs is the most common way companies attempt to make change. Once again, these

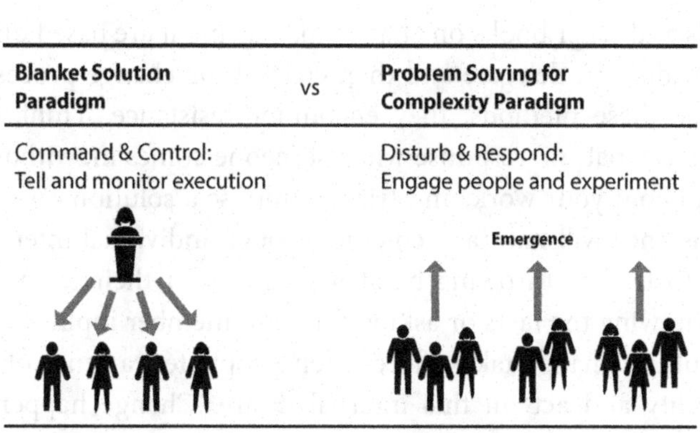

FIGURE 5.4
A Comparison of Handling Change Assumptions.

programs are top-down, usually delegated, and sometimes managed by external consulting firms. The leader does not get intimately engaged in the program and does not question his or her leadership role in the culture change process.

OVERVIEW

There are many articles and books on change management, but nearly all of them are rooted in the Imposing Blanket Solutions paradigm. They offer a prescriptive set of steps to follow in order to make the change. For example, John Kotter's *Leading Change* describes, chapter by chapter, an approach driven by leadership.

Successful change, in Kotter's book, is described as an 8-step process:

1. Create a sense of urgency
2. Build a guiding coalition
3. Form a strategic vision and initiatives
4. Communicate the change vision
5. Enlist a volunteer army
6. Enable action by removing barriers
7. Generate short-term wins
8. Institute change

Kotter's and other books on change management are based on the idea that the leader can delegate and then control the change process. When leaders use these methods, they encounter resistance. Think about it. Resistance is a natural response when someone comes in, without knowing much about your work, and tries to impose a solution on your work plan. Resistance will naturally emerge through individual interactions in response to leaders throwing blanket solutions at their team members without knowing the facts or asking for team member input.

True culture change takes place when people feel a sense of personal responsibility and act on this internal desire. Change happens in the context of complex adaptive systems, not static mechanical systems.

CONNECTION TO OTHER ASSUMPTIONS

The third of the five assumptions, how we think about change, builds on the two assumptions covered above. If your worldview is reductionist, where the organization is fragmented and made of separate parts, then your management approach can only be about attempting to control the parts by imposing a common set of new rules and rolling out programs.

However, if you have a systems worldview, then you can see how the organization interacts with the world around it. Your focus becomes how to create value to your customers or perhaps value in your community. The role of the leader is to build problem-solving teams that excel at improving value delivery in a model where people work together at solving system problems. The role of the leader is to create the conditions for *problem solving, self-organization, and emergence* to take place. These, again, are characteristics of complex adaptive systems.

BACKGROUND

We have a long history of command and control management. During the middle ages, feudalism was a social system where two groups of people were committed to each other. The vassals made a commitment to their lord, usually in the form of military service, and in return, they were given "fiefs" or parcels of land so they could become more self-sufficient. The lord commanded where and when the vassal needed to engage in battle to protect the kingdom.

Once the industrial revolution began, the command-and-control model continued. The owner of the company expected specific tasks to be performed by the employees per his/her instructions. Later, Henry Ford and his employees adopted the command-and-control management structure where the employees were not expected (or respected enough) to think. Their job was to simply execute the commands of the supervisor.

Let's think about how change takes place. Most organizations are still rolling out blanket solutions for culture change. We both have been working with companies for nearly two decades and have seen one consistent pattern of how leaders think about change. They all want the "program": "Give me the step-by-step, easy-to-understand version of how to make change happen." So many people believe there are phases to the change program, and leaders and teams need to move carefully from one phase to the next. People think measuring success is about identifying the principles and characteristics and then doing either a self-assessment or have someone outside the company come and ask questions. People approach change with a top-down rollout and control-the-parts mentality. What we're proposing in this book is a totally different organic approach to change that we'll cover in Part 3, Action. The model we use is based on building new thinking and habits from the bottom-up, allowing the organization to grow and create helpful "disturbances" where needed.

A BRIEF REVIEW

The Limiting Effects of Command and Control

- Allows people to avoid taking personal responsibility for problems
- Limits effective problem resolution by focusing only on completing tasks for the boss
- Creates non-value-added tasks by having multiple reviews of presentations that will satisfy the boss

- Prevents the adaptability of the team to respond to emerging problems
- Gives employees a reduced sense of value

The Positive Effects of Self-Organization and Emergence

- Engages people at higher levels of ownership with intrinsic motivation
- Enables the collective creativity of the people
- Allows for changes to plan with rapid responses
- Encourages continuous development of system problem-solving capabilities
- Enables development of employee skills

OK, let's reflect! Are you operating under the command and control model? Do you roll out orders? Do you have goals deployed to all the functions without checking for achievability? Do you feel like your role is above others? Do you often model good problem-solving skills and practices? How much of your daily effort is in developing your employees?

SOCIAL CONNECTIONS: DEFENSIVE REASONING VERSUS INTERNALIZATION

What Is the Best Way to Interact with Other People?

Chuck, a plant manager I (Jim) knew once, became aware that a customer had a failure of a product from his plant. Before reading the defect report or even seeing the part, he sent an email to the senior leadership team proclaiming that the failure was the result of a design problem created by the engineering department and not a manufacturing issue.

Blaming someone else was Chuck's normal response to problems. How often have you heard someone in your organization say, "If you want to solve this problem, you need to talk to someone else"? This is a frequent knee-jerk reaction to problems that we have observed in so, so many companies.

Blanket Solution Paradigm	VS	Problem Solving for Complexity Paradigm
Defensive Reasoning: Blame others 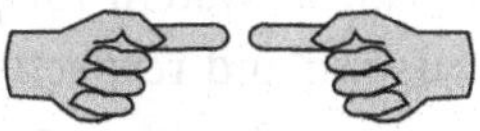		Internalization: Trust and respect others 

FIGURE 5.5
A Comparison of Social Connections Assumptions.

OVERVIEW

The fourth category of assumptions exposes the deeply held beliefs we have about how we need to interact with other people. There are three forms of communication: Dictate, Debate, and Dialogue (which you will read more about in Action). *Dictate* is where one person tells the other what to do. *Debate* is the form of communication where each person has a perspective, believes his/her perspective is right, and then defends that perspective. *Dialogue* is where the two people actively listen to each other, work at trying to understand the other person's thinking, and then combine the thinking of both so that a new view of the problem can emerge. It is fundamentally respectful and is the only method of communication we've seen work to solve problems. It works because it builds trust, every step of the way.

CONNECTION TO OTHER ASSUMPTIONS

Building on the previous assumption categories, organizations operating under the Imposing Blanket Solutions paradigm, because of their fragmented and individualist mindset, tend to allow blame between people and functions. When your company is fragmented, and each person and function is expected to achieve their own objectives, there is a natural tendency to blame other parts of the system. The alternative paradigm, Problem Solving for Complexity, is about solving system problems together and openly looking for solutions to problems by examining the interactions between the parts. This paradigm requires an open and honest way of communicating, without blame and with maximum respect for the other person's perspective.

An organization needs safety built into its social system for people to be able to expose real problems. Having a trusting and respectful culture is key to exposing problems and engaging everyone in getting to the root cause of problems. Once you make the transition to a system worldview where all the parts and individuals, are interdependent, then removing the fear is key. It allows people start exposing and solving problems naturally because they feel safe and genuinely curious about what's going on where the problems are taking place.

BACKGROUND

We need to talk about defensive reasoning as a habit if we're going to talk about blame. In 1990, Chris Argyris published a book, *Overcoming Organizational Defenses: Facilitating Organizational Learning.* He describes what he calls defensive reasoning and explains how it severely inhibits organizational learning. In essence, defensive reasoning is a protection mechanism where an individual or a group blames someone else for problems in order to avoid feeling embarrassed or being shamed. When we see this habit in organizations, we might describe it as a blame culture. Blame cultures tend to emerge in highly fragmented organizations that have a big focus on attaining goals at the function, group, or individual level. If we're used to working in blame cultures, creating new habits around how to interact with others just takes some practice.

A STORY ABOUT USING INQUIRY FOR BUILDING TRUST

Several years ago, I (still Jim here) went through some training at GISC, The Gestalt International Study Center on Cape Cod. Their model for leadership is consistent with everything we're talking about in regard to Problem Solving for Complexity. Specifically, the idea that the role of the leader is to create collective energy among people by facilitating group dialogue to solve problems.

At GISC, we had a training exercise where we worked in groups of six with each person taking on the position of leader and facilitating the whole group in solving a problem. As a leader, we were each instructed to not assert our own opinions, but instead, pay attention to the back and forth communications between team members. When it was my turn to lead, I was careful to thank people for their contributions and make sure all people participated equally. With only 5 minutes left to go in the exercise, I began to summarize their great work. At this point, Sonia Nevis, the workshop facilitator, walked through the circle directly toward me and asked, "Why did you do that? Did you notice how the energy left the room as soon as you started talking?"

Being caught in that moment had a profound impact on me. I learned that the role of the leader is to build trust, model dialogue, and build energy. By inserting myself in the group dialogue rather than paying attention to their energy, I undermined the process of building trust. I did not support inquiry throughout the exercise. I am still practicing how to quit thinking about the problem and instead pay attention to the social dynamics inside the group. I am learning to always be curious about how others are thinking. I am learning to respect and trust others and suspect I will always be learning this.

A BRIEF REVIEW

The Limiting Effects of Defensive Reasoning

- Allows people to not take personal responsibility for problems
- Limits effective problem resolution by focusing only on one function at a time
- Restricts effective dialogue for system problem-solving
- Builds barriers between functions and reinforces the fragmented worldview
- Allows ineffective communication that diminishes trust and respect

The Positive Effects of Internalization

- Enables the collective creativity of the organization's resources
- Allows people to solve complex problems
- Encourages continuous development of system problem-solving capabilities
- Enables development of employee skills

This time we need to think about your communication style. What percent of the time do you think the problem is "out there" and belongs to someone else: employee, function, customer? How often do you communicate this to your employees? When do you accept responsibility for problems and ask yourself, "I wonder how I might have contributed to the problem?" What type of communication do you observe, dictation, debate, or dialogue?

 ## CREATING KNOWLEDGE: KNOWERS VERSUS LEARNERS

What Do We Believe to Be True about Knowledge and Learning?

Richard Feynman, the theoretical physicist well known for his work in quantum mechanics and particle physics, tells a story about his early childhood. He remembered as a child walking through the woods with his friend, his friend's father, and his father. His friend was able to name all the birds, trees, and flowers, and Richard could not do that. Instead, Richard's father asked him questions like, "Why does that bird have that shaped beak or why are the feathers that color?"

Richard was given a gift from his father to stay curious and ask deeper questions about the nature of life. Richard was a learner and his friend was a knower.

OVERVIEW

The final category of assumptions concerns our beliefs about knowledge: whether we believe that knowledge is something essentially fixed

Blanket Solution Paradigm	vs	Problem Solving for Complexity Paradigm
Knower: Provide answers		Learner: Seek answers from others

FIGURE 5.6
A Comparison of Creating Knowledge Assumptions.

once we have acquired it, or whether knowledge is flexible and fluid, shifting, and changing over time. We will look at knowledge vs. learning at the personal and the organizational level.

Carol Dweck, author of *The Growth Mindset*, defines two different mindsets, fixed and growth. People who think they know everything they need to know already tend to have a fixed mindset and people who believe they are capable of continuously learning tend to have a growth mindset.

"Knower-leaders" severely limit the natural process of learning for their teams. As a leader, every time you offer a solution or dictate next steps, you take back the ownership of the problem from the person you are trying to lead and support. If you ever say, "Bring me the data!", you are positioning yourself as the knower and your people can't help but allow you to own the problem now. But if we start from the assumption that problems are not completely knowable given their inevitable complexity, we can more easily maintain the state of being a learner while guiding others in effective problem-solving.

BACKGROUND

Most of us have been raised to be knowers. Starting in grade school, so many of us were expected to memorize facts and recall these facts on tests. We were rewarded for our "knowledge" with the high grades we received. Becoming a learner takes some effort to divert our thinking from what we know to what we don't know.

In his article, "Confessions of a Recovering Knower," Brian Hinken challenges us to ask ourselves if the knower impulse is limiting us. He addresses what it means to be a knower versus a learner. Leaders, he says, are more likely to be knowers than learners because of the cultural expectations of most companies. People are usually promoted for *knowing* their functional area and their ability to provide solutions to their problems. But leaders who act as a knower limit their ability to accomplish what is important for themselves and their organization. They create limited engagement.

Leaders who are learners engage with people differently listening to all points of view, allowing team members to agree on an approach that arises from the collective understanding of the problem situation. As a result, employees are naturally more excited about their work. Teams become more dedicated to understanding and solving the problems when a leader is curious about what they are doing and learning.

Olga and I have had the opportunity to go into many companies, large and small, across nearly every industry to work with people on building problem-solving teams. Generally, the process involves (1) defining business problems with leaders, (2) scoping projects with managers and value stream owners, (3) engaging teams in defining problems, designing a future state, and creating a plan to be executed in monthly cycles. During this process, senior leaders are brought into the room to observe and assess the team's progress on building new process for improvement. For most leaders, the natural response is to judge the progress, offer a perspective of what needs to be done, and walk out of the room. We do some coaching with leaders before reviews, suggesting that they ask open-ended questions, and try not to interfere with the learning the team has been exposed to at solving the problem. And with some leaders, it works. But with most leaders, they still feel a need to offer their solutions to the problem. For many leaders, the knower pops up so much more often than the learner. It's a human habit. Becoming a learner, requires intention, awareness, and you guessed it . . . *practice*.

A BRIEF REVIEW

The Limiting Effects of Knowers

- Limiting throughput by restricting decision-making to the knower

- Having ineffective communications, either debate or dictation, which limits getting the needed information required to expose the root cause
- Reduces trust and respect with their employees
- Limits looking at creative alternatives vs. getting stuck on the one known solution

The Positive Effects of Becoming a Learner

- Creates a focus on the details of a problem with open communications
- Allows people to solve complex problems
- Encourages continuous development of system problem-solving capabilities
- Enables development of employee skills

Final reflection. Do you need to be right in conversation with others? Do you work at convincing people to accept your thinking? Or, are you curious about problem situations, asking others how they are seeing things? Do you integrate different perspectives to get a more complete understanding of the situation at hand?

Review Figure 5.1 for the complete model that includes the assumptions for both paradigms. We hope you will find it useful in your culture change process.

In this chapter, we have covered five sets of assumptions for each of the two paradigms. Think of these as guideposts as you shift paradigms. We have a few more things to cover before we start working on culture change. In the next section, we'll talk about connecting new assumptions to actions you can take to help transition your organization to the new paradigm, Problem Solving for Complexity.

Part 3

Action

Rapid Learning Experiments to Move an Organization from Imposing Blanket Solutions to the Culture of Problem Solving for Complexity

Reading the previous chapters, you must have mumbled a few times, "OK, so what? What am I going to *do* with all this information?" We hope to answer this question for you in this section because everything in it is about *doing*.

In our Transformational Leadership workshop, when we observed leaders working together to solve business problems, we were excited to see a steady pattern of connectivity between the results they produced and their ability to self-organize and form adaptive teams that could solve complex problems.

Self-organization is important in order for leaders to be able to deliver on the following "leadership actions":

- Define problems *at the point of delivery to the customer* and deploy the problem-solving responsibility to the right person (which makes work simpler and less confusing)
- Demonstrate an ability to communicate in a respectful, non-judgmental way to gain a better understanding of cross-functional problems (which takes advantage of everybody's good thinking and contributions to the problem-solving process)
- Initiate a non-threatening follow-up process as a way of sharing the learning that results from individual and team problem-solving efforts (which creates the conditions for continuous learning)

Then we began to look for this pattern in our consulting and coaching engagements, too. We discovered that these actions consistently produced better outcomes because they helped create an environment that supported the ability of team members to focus on the customer, adjust on a fly if customer requirements changed, allocate resources in the most effective way possible, and generate a lot of new knowledge during their problem-solving work ... new knowledge that could then be shared to improve other business processes.

Then we learned something else. These three actions could be traced back to one or several assumptions of the Problem Solving for Complexity paradigm. In this part of the book, we explore each of the above leadership actions and their linkage to the leadership assumptions.

	Assumptions	Actions
	Focus on results	Build the Framework for Problem Solving (Chapter 6)
	System worldview	
	Disturb and respond	
	Internalize	Grow Respectful Social Connections (Chapter 7))
	Be a learner	Accelerate Organizational Learning (Chapter 8)

FIGURE 6.1
How Actions Relate to Assumptions.

The first chapter, *"Build a Framework for Problem Solving,"* describes what leaders can do to overcome the fragmented, functional organizational structure, which makes it difficult to define problems of cross-functional processes that create and deliver value to external customers. We introduce an approach for helping leaders and teams across functions to understand value-stream problems and build a *structure for collaborative problem-solving*. These actions are driven by the assumptions associated with Leadership Attention, Worldview, and How Change Happens.

In the second chapter, *"Grow Respectful Social Connections,"* we describe exactly this: how leaders create an environment of safety, trust, and mutual accountability through intentionally respectful connections with everyone. We'll talk about how through attentive listening, humble inquiry, and dialogue, leaders can build open lines of communication growing better relationships and patterns that make for a healthier organization. By modeling these actions and coaching others to practice them, leaders shift away from the blame culture and defensive reasoning. Instead, they begin to *internalize* their responsibility for identifying and addressing problems at their root cause and supporting problem-solving efforts at every organizational level and across functions.

In the third and final chapter, *"Accelerate Organizational Learning,"* our intention is to introduce you to practices that help move each person in your company, including you, from being *a knower* to *a learner*. This chapter is about what you can do to create an organization of learners.

These three leadership actions, applied together, can help transition you and your organization from the Imposing Blanket Solutions paradigm to the Problem Solving for Complexity paradigm. All three actions reinforce each other, so leaders need to practice them simultaneously. Showing preference for just one or two of these actions will almost surely lead to an imbalance between the technical and social aspects of your transformation. It will also get in the way of your company's ability to adapt to change and appropriately respond to problems and learn.

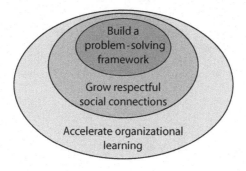

FIGURE 6.2
Leadership Actions in Support of Paradigm Transformation.

Only by practicing all three actions simultaneously—*building a framework for problem solving, growing respectful social connections, and accelerating organizational learning*—will you work effectively with complex adaptive systems to make a sustainable long-term impact on your organization's ability to solve problems and thrive.

6

Build a Framework for Problem Solving

> *"Don't focus on culture because culture is a bottomless pit and can be a big waste of time. Just get your people involved in working on the solution to your business problem. If you don't have time for that, you are in trouble."*
> Edgar Schein

Companies, if they were allowed to self-organize, would just turn into complex adaptive systems, with individuals and teams inside them able to quickly adapt to external changes producing results that would exceed any CEO's expectations. However, the organizational structure, in most companies, is vertical, i.e. composed of individual functions and departments (silos!), which creates separation and a sense of false independence. Department heads tend to see each other as rivals and prevent any attempt at crossing functional barriers.

In a vertical organization, targets and performance metrics are set within individual departments, processes are designed with little or no regard to how they affect adjacent steps, and leadership development focuses on serving the needs of functional silos instead of building critical capabilities that the whole company needs in order to achieve its priorities. Last but not least, problem solving within individual functions leads to sub-optimization of functional processes and generation of problems at handoffs between functions. And while all this work inside vertical siloes keeps them busy, it doesn't change the outputs of the overall value stream, producing no benefits for the end customer!

In a contrast to an imposed-from-the-top vertical organizational structure, a process for creating and delivering customer value (also known as a "value stream") cuts *across* functional silos until it reaches the end customer. Which is why, when you want to learn how to solve problems effectively, your first step is help people see *value streams,* understand how they perform, and take a swift decisive action at the first sight of problems that affect value-stream performance.

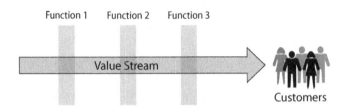

FIGURE 6.3
Organizational Value Stream.

Most companies have primary value streams, i.e. the processes that are directly responsible for the delivery to the end customer (Operations, Sales, Distribution, Product Development), and secondary value streams, i.e. internal processes that exist to support the primary value streams (Finance, Legal, IT, Human Resources, etc.). The process for designing, supporting, and continuously improving value streams is the same, both for primary and secondary value streams. The only difference is that the primary value streams are built with the end customer in mind, while the purpose of secondary value streams is to enable primary value streams do their job.

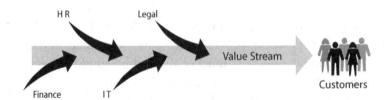

FIGURE 6.4
Primary and Secondary Value Streams.

Value-stream thinking eliminates unnecessary complexity, which helps everyone in an organization align around a common goal of serving the end customer. It reduces competition between functions and encourages collaboration. It supports the ability of teams to self-organize and focus on the problems that hurt value-creating process.

Having explained the merits of value-stream thinking, let's talk about the process of leading individuals and teams to solve value-stream problems.

EVERY VALUE STREAM HAS PROBLEMS TO BE SOLVED

Let's be clear: a business only exists because there exists a customer who is willing to purchase its product or service. Actually, ANY organization, for-profit or non-profit, exists because someone (company, group, or individuals) is interested in what it has to offer. We will continue using terms like "customer," "business process," and "business results" in this book, but we encourage you to think about their application beyond a business context.

What differentiates a successful company from the rest of the pack is an ability to deliver to the customer *exactly what they need, at the precise time when they need it.* This ability depends on how quickly and effectively an organization can remove obstacles that interfere with the flow of value to the customer. A leader's job in the Problem Solving for Complexity paradigm is to help team members do this.

An underlying condition for creating the process for solving value-stream problems is two-fold:

a) Understand what **VALUE** customers (external or internal) seek in the product or service delivered by a value stream, and

b) Create **METRICS** to measure value-stream outputs vs. customer requirements

Customer Requirements
- Quality
- Quantity
- Timeliness
- Price
- Safety

Performance Metrics
- Percentage C&A
- Number of units
- Lead time
- Cost
- Recordable accidents

Customers

FIGURE 6.5
Measuring Value-Stream Outputs vs. Customer Requirements.

Don't overcomplicate metrics! Most customer requirements are related to one or some (or all) of the following criteria: *Quality/Quantity/Price/Timely Delivery/Safety*. Of course, what quality means in, say, a dentist's practice is different from how customers of a construction company think about quality. A drive-through customer in a fast food restaurant expects an order to be delivered in a matter of seconds, while someone who ordered custom-made kitchen cabinets doesn't mind a 3-month waiting time. Your value-stream metrics need to reflect the nature of your company's product/service and should be developed to track your ability to satisfy the unique needs of YOUR customers.

Once you are clear on the customer requirements and have metrics developed, it is time to start building the process for solving value-stream problems:

Step One: If metrics show a discrepancy between customer requirements and value-stream outputs AT THE POINT OF DELIVERY TO THE CUSTOMER, define the GAP (problem) in specific measurable terms.

Step Two: Once the gap is defined, assign OWNERSHIP for this problem.

Step Three: Analyze work inside the value stream or at points of delivery by secondary value streams, and find problems that CONTRIBUTE to the gap.

Step Four: Assign OWNERS to each contributing problem. Form problem-solving teams (this work requires collaboration).

Step Five: Find ROOT CAUSES for contributing problems through RAPID LEARNING EXPERIMENTS.

Step Six: Design EXPERIMENTS to propose and test COUNTER-MEASURES. Assess the effectiveness of countermeasures and decide which should be implemented as permanent solutions.

Step Seven: Implement SOLUTIONS.

Step Eight: REFLECT on the process. Capture LEARNING from the problem-solving effort and share with the rest of the organization.

Note that steps 5–7 are usually accomplished through multiple PDCA cycles. This is where problem-solving teams engage in

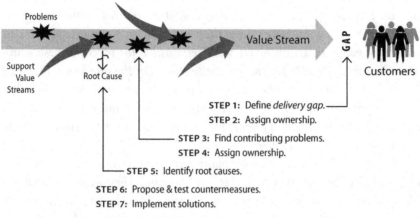

FIGURE 6.6
Process for Solving Value-Stream Problems.

ongoing experimentation, learning, and continuous improvement to close problem gaps. (We will elaborate on this in Chapter 8.)

Let's take a deeper dive into each step of the problem-solving process. To illustrate the process, we will use a case study. We created it on the basis of our consulting engagement with a company that decided to make a shift from Imposing Blanket Solutions to Problem Solving for Complexity.

Case Study: Company/Problem Overview

This company runs a very successful high-volume business providing food products to grocery stores and restaurants in the United States. They have three plants, each producing a different product mix to their customers.

The major business challenge that the company had faced for years was that their products were commodities and in order to either maintain or improve their market position and survive with other players in this market, they needed to constantly increase their production volume while keeping costs as low as possible.

At the end of each year, executives held meetings to create a plan for the upcoming year. A common practice was to use performance results of *the current year to establish goals for the next year. The focus typically was on the increase in sales and cost reduction. Each functional department received new budgets (lower than last year) along with specific cost reduction goals. Function heads were responsible for meeting these goals. Manufacturing usually got the most attention. On the one hand, they had to commit to certain production growth targets; on the other hand, they were responsible for a high percentage of the total spending of the company. This is why every year, plant managers were typically required to reduce costs by $1M each.*

Having received their targets, plant managers would meet with their teams to develop the plan for achieving the goal. They would brainstorm ideas, agree on the list, add up the expected savings, and then finalize their list of projects (solutions) that were supposed to help increase production and deliver the desired cost savings. Typically, solutions were geared toward equipment upgrades, management of material costs, and headcount reductions.

The list of projects would then be given to Finance for keeping track of production and actual versus projected costs. On a monthly basis, Finance would generate reports and present them to the senior leaders in a review meeting where the plant managers reported on their plant performance. Every time they failed to achieve their targets, they were required to explain why they were behind.

The process was clearly based on the assumptions of the Imposing Blanket Solutions paradigm. It was so frustrating for everybody involved that finally the company decided that something needed to change.

Jim was asked to work as a coach for the director of operations to structure an intervention that would help initiate the shift from their current Imposing Blanket Solutions paradigm to a Problem Solving for Complexity paradigm. The plan was to change the focus from financial goals (results) to the improvement of their value streams (means) in order to achieve production growth and cost savings goals. The first step was to define a problem (a gap) in value-stream performance.

Let's pause for a moment to talk about defining performance gaps at the point of delivery to the end customer. Again, when companies operate in a vertically structured world—with the process for creating customer value going across different functions and/or departments— team members have to deal with lots of conflicting, confusing, and complicated information and situations ... especially when it comes to problem solving. What do you think happens when silos take action to improve functional outputs?

Let's say, a Call Center in an insurance company decides to reduce the time operators spend on calls with customers when they call to report an accident and initiate a claim. In itself, this isn't a bad idea. Nobody likes to be held on the phone for too long, especially if you just had an accident and feel stressed and rattled. However, the shorter the call time, the less information an operator is able to obtain from the customer, which is why the Call Center needs to check with the Claims department (the next step in the value-stream) on what information they need for efficient claim processing. But in a rigid world where silos focus only on their own work and don't talk to each other, this just doesn't happen. The Call Center introduces a new and improved operator script and celebrates productivity gains. The Claim's process in the meantime gets more complicated because claims reps have to make additional calls to customers to obtain information they no longer receive from the Call Center. The overall performance of the value stream doesn't get better and customers still get phone calls, just from other people. Plus Claims now holds a grudge against the Call Center, not a fertile ground for any future collaboration.

In short, solving problems within functional siloes creates bigger downstream problems, complicating relationships between departments while the end customer gains nothing. An organization that wants to reduce complexity and increase its ability to adapt and improve needs to use a value-stream perspective when attempting to identify problems.

Now, back to the case study.

Dig into the Work Inside Value Streams to Find Contributing Problems

Plant managers who owned manufacturing value streams needed to understand what gaps in value-stream performance contributed to the high-level business problem of insufficient production growth and high operating cost. To get a better grasp of the problem situation, they studied value-stream performance for the past several years and spend quite a bit of time talking to operators and supervisors in production, maintenance, and other areas to get their perspective on the situation.

Notice the hands-on nature of the work that led them to understand and define the problem. Some companies that aspire to create the culture of Problem Solving for Complexity *while still operating with an Imposing Blanket Solutions mindset* believe that problems can be solved merely with "collaborative thinking." We have each witnessed many teams in conference rooms debating problems and potential solutions. They analyze staggering amounts of data, review numerous reports, and "brainstorm," all without ever leaving the conference room.

But Problem Solving for Complexity—and this is where Lean thinking and practice has been so helpful—is based on grasping the facts of the problem situation. And the only place where one can grasp the facts and see what is happening first-hand is the workplace, where customer value is created. You, as a leader, need to role model this behavior. So get out of your office and go see your team! You will be amazed how much you will learn by simply talking to people and observing their work.

Back to our story.

*The plant managers learned that the main problem manufacturing faced was downtime. It affected throughput and increased production costs. They calculated that if they could reduce downtime from 4 to 2 hours per week, they could achieve their production growth and cost reduction targets. Getting down to this simple and tangible problem statement—**eliminating 2 hours of downtime**—helped get rid of the "noise" and create a razor-sharp focus on the target. Everyone, including the teams and functions that were organizationally disconnected from manufacturing, could now focus on processes inside their own value streams that contributed to the downtime problem and take action to resolve process issues.*

Overall, there were seven functions that owned support value streams. Not unlike in most companies, these groups weren't really aware that manufacturing was their internal customer, hence not being sure of how and when they needed to deliver value to the primary value stream. Developing primary and support value-stream awareness was key to building a framework for Problem Solving for Complexity.

To transition from the current state to the future state, leaders created a plan and outlined the following expected outcomes:

- *All three plants would begin to work on the improvement of the process flow focusing on downtime reduction.*
- *All functions, inside and outside of manufacturing, would focus on the delivery of value to the primary value stream and take action to understand their contribution to the downtime gap.*
- *All groups would use weekly PDCA cycles to drive real-time implementation and learning.*
- *All groups would learn how to conduct deep reflection sessions each month for self-correction and continuous improvement.*

Plant managers took the ownership of the downtime problem at their respective plants, and the owner of each support function accepted responsibility for identifying and solving problems in the delivery of their value streams to manufacturing.

It is the rule of thumb that *whoever owns the point of delivery to the customer, owns the problem.* Does this mean that he or she must solve it single-handedly? Of course not! Problem solving is almost always a collaborative effort that requires participation of multiple stakeholders, but it is the responsibility of the problem owner to identify those who need to be on the team and lead them through the problem-solving process.

The next step in this problem-solving effort was a five-day intervention that brought together representative of all plants' functions and helped develop a common focus and the sense of purpose. On day one, plant managers defined their downtime goals and representatives from support functions defined their points of contribution to the primary value stream. During the next three days, support functions designed their future-state value streams and reviewed improvement plans with leadership. On the final day of the intervention, all groups created 30-day implementation plans and scheduled weekly PDCA* sessions to review progress and made adjustments as needed.

Collaborative problem-solving efforts led by plant managers helped teams find a number of contributing problems that led to downtime: materials (packages, labels) were not available when needed, there was a

---

* We introduced the scientific method of PDCA in the chapter on Paradigms. Further on, when we will discuss your role in building a non-threatening follow-up process to engage your organization in continuous learning from its problem-solving effort, we will elaborate on the application of rapid PDCA cycles to foster learning and continuous improvement.

shortage of qualified people to perform certain operations, machines often malfunctioned and needed to be serviced, rapid/frequent schedule changes caused additional changeover time, etc.

Continue Digging to Identify Root Causes

Once all contributing problems were identified, teams began to search for root causes. They discovered that it was corrugated box humidity variation that caused machines to stop. HR, by not providing timely training to manufacturing, caused personnel shortages. Quality checks disrupted a process flow, which in turn caused delays. Material movement didn't take into consideration the capacity of individual machines. Scheduling was allowing too many changeovers during runs, which affected the production flow. And maintenance wasn't ordering replacement parts in needed quantities.

You'll notice that the search for root causes is absolutely not a linear process. It involves *rapid learning experimentation* (quick PDCA cycles), which allows problem-solving teams quickly move from a hypothesis to testing to confirmation. If you don't test your hypothesis about what causes the problem, you risk spending time, money, and effort to develop a solution just to discover later that the problem reoccurs (because again, the solution doesn't target the real cause of the problem).

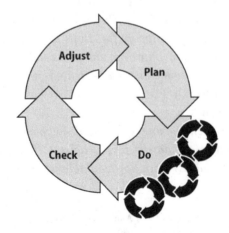

FIGURE 6.7
Rapid Learning Experiments Inside the PDCA Cycle.

You will want to use rapid learning experimentation when you get to selecting countermeasures as well. Don't spend too much time trying to develop a perfect solution. Instead, propose several counter-measures and come up with ways to test them ... quickly and inexpensively. Not only will you zoom in on the best solution to your problem in a short period of time, you and your team will also learn a lot as you move from one experiment to another. Your job as a leader is to model this approach for other leaders within the organization.

Learning to Learn through Problem Solving

The key to the success of their problem-solving effort was the ability of teams to conduct regular structured reflection sessions to check on the progress and to capture lessons in the process. Besides weekly reflections, every 30 days, groups got together for an even deeper reflection to be able to create a plan for the following month. The framework for reflection was created by these simple questions (feel free to use them with your team):

- *What did we plan?*
- *What did we do?*
- *What worked?*
- *What didn't work?*
- *What did we learn:*
  - *About the problem*
  - *About our ability to use PDCA as a driver for problem-solving work?*

By practicing reflection, teams learned many lessons that that they applied to improve processes in their value streams:

Quality: Schedule quality checks to minimize disruption to the manu-facturing flow and help reduce downtime.

Purchasing: Go beyond product specs and involve suppliers to help solve downtime issues caused by their products.

HR: Structure the hiring process and develop training programs to help maintain better flow in manufacturing.

Scheduling: Improve daily planning to keep the lines from being disrupted by sales emergencies.

Finance: Share information about daily performance with the plants before they start their shift. This can help the plants create more consistent daily plans.

Maintenance: Improve the availability of replacement parts for the machines so when a part goes bad, it can be replaced more quickly, thus reducing downtime.

Materials Management: Get synchronized with the daily schedules and pre-plan each day to assure all materials are available to each department, on time, in the right quantity.

One of the main lessons learned by all participating teams was about the power of value-stream thinking. As Jim hoped, they discovered that this created alignment between functions inside the company and helped expedite the improvement process, make it more robust and effective. Within three months, downtime reduction targets were either achieved or within reach. Plant teams and function teams developed a habit for collaborative problem solving. Functions learned that the plants were their customers and they needed to deliver value to the plants at the right place at the right time to improve their throughput.

Using a value-stream lens to solve business problems is the first step in building the foundation of the Problem-Solving framework. Disrupting a traditional top-down goal deployment process and engaging teams in solving problems *at the point of delivery to the end customer* is what helps you shift from the Imposing Blanket Solutions paradigm to Problem Solving for Complexity. By removing functional barriers, encouraging collaborative problem solving, and allowing people to take ownership of value-stream problems, you unleash the power of complex adaptive systems inside your company ... and your ability to work within the complex adaptive world beyond your company's doors.

Next, we will describe the social component of the Problem Solving for Complexity paradigm, namely, how leaders contribute to building respectful connections between people in the problem-solving process. We will discuss how you can model communication that shows respect for people's ability to solve problems, and how you can create an environment of trust where people want to take ownership of solving problems.

7

Grow Respectful Social Connections

"When people honor each other, there is a trust established that leads to synergy, interdependence, and deep respect. Both parties make decisions and choices based on what is right, what is best, and what is valued most highly."

Blaine Lee

STRONG SOCIAL CONNECTIONS ARE ABOUT CURIOSITY AND TRUST

Imagine an organization of problem solvers, in which people at all levels are able to rapidly respond to the complex adaptive world, meeting the needs of their customers and stakeholders, and contributing to the community . . .

Imagine people working together, across functions, energized by challenge, having fun, enjoying being a part of a diverse team . . .

Imagine team members not obsessively thinking whether or not they will get the credit or who is to blame for mistakes . . .

Imagine managers honoring their direct reports by wanting them to pursue their own higher purpose and see them succeed, respecting their wisdom . . .

Imagine new employees being integrated into the organization with appreciation, following standards developed with the intent of learning by the existing teams, but not being afraid to take ownership of problems or share ideas with enthusiasm?

How many companies do you know that operate this way?

In the last chapter, we introduced a process for building the Framework for Problem Solving by aligning people to serve value to the customer. This chapter adds the social component of team-based problem solving that helps organizations solve problems that exist in our complex adaptive world. The types of problems we face in the workplace require people work together, combining different perspectives and skills, and co-developing solutions to the root causes of the problems.

Effective communication skills that honor and respect the thinking of others are key for effective problem solving. You, as the leader, understand the importance of modeling the problem-solving process because you are aware of your influence and that you are being watched and copied.

In this chapter, we talk about how you can model an effective communication style, one that inspires people, builds trust, and creates a respectful culture. And even if you feel confident about your ability to communicate effectively, we know these practices can help. As you lead through these intentional communication practices, your organization will come alive, respectful social connections will emerge, and a self-organizing, adaptive problem-solving culture will start to grow. People copy people, especially leaders. And it's almost always about how we talk to each other.

So, to start, let's look at an example of an exchange between the members of a leadership team.

In the scene below, we reconstruct a conversation that took place in a meeting inside the simulation in our Transformational Leadership Program. The "CEO" called this meeting with the intent to hear from his "direct reports" about how they propose to improve company performance.

CEO:	*"I just looked at the latest financial report and saw that our profits keep trending down for the year. The next BOD meeting is in two weeks, and I need to prepare a response about how we are going to improve our performance and show the Board better numbers."*
CFO:	*"I hope you all received my memo about the need to increase prices to improve our profits. The faster we get this implemented, the better off we will be."*
VP of Sales:	*"And I already responded to your memo. Raising prices will kill sales. We are losing volume because of slow response to customer inquiries, especially in our service business. We have competitors waiting in the*

	wings to take our business and a price increase will make things worse."
VP of Operations:	"Please don't make Operations a scapegoat for all our problems! We can't respond to customer inquiries in time because our IT system is archaic."
CIO:	"Here we go! How many times have I raised this issue already? We all know our current system is holding us behind. Let's make a quick decision on the supplier for a new IT system and get things running."
VP of HR:	"I know it doesn't answer your question, but we do need to complete performance evaluations by the end of this quarter. I asked each of you to provide dates for your performance reviews but didn't get any responses. Do we have to have this conversation every year?!"
CEO:	"The BOD will sure be happy to hear we got performance reviews done. Would you mind taking this issue out of this meeting? We have some more important problems to investigate.
	I think we definitely need to consider increasing prices. We haven't done it for a long time, so I am sure Sales will find ways to justify it to customers. However, I also want us to talk about the merger that we've been pondering for a while. I believe it is the most optimal way to improve our financial performance."

What do you see in this conversation? There's a lot going on in this quick exchange.

To start, these folks are not attentively listening to each other; all they want is to bring up issues they believe matter most from their perspective. Each person is locked into his/her idea and is trying to influence others. The debate continues as each person attempts to reinforce their perspective. There's a lot of finger pointing going on inside this conversation, too. Function Heads are not going to admit they may be responsible for the decline in profits and are more than ready to blame others for poor performance.

Finally, we are sure you noticed how CEO dominates the conversation. He calls the meeting to hear his Function Heads' perspective on the company problems. Instead, it turns out he has already formed an opinion and selected a solution that, in his mind, should help solve the profitability problem. Also, he entirely dismisses the attempt by the VP of HR to raise an issue of performance reviews. This may not be directly linked to the problem of declining profits, but it is clearly one of the procedures that touches each company employee and cannot be simply put aside for the sake of other matters.

This scene demonstrates just one of the scenarios that took place in the Transformational Leadership Program. What all these scenarios have in common is the lack of desire to build an effective communication *process* in which each participant is heard and every contribution is respected. In such a process, the idea is that decisions are made based on a thorough understanding of the problems at hand and team members (with the help of a good leader) have made a mutual agreement to prioritize them in a way that makes most sense for the company and its customers.

We're used to thinking in terms of processes when it comes to products and services, but effective communication requires a process, too. We dramatically improve the health of teams and organizations when we pay attention to communication processes and model this attention for others.

WHY PROBLEM SOLVING FOR COMPLEXITY REQUIRES SPECIFIC COMMUNICATION SKILLS

There are three major reasons for improving our communications skills in order to be able to create the culture of Problem Solving for Complexity:

First, the *problems are too complex* to be solved by one individual. Creating clarity of the problem situation requires looking at the system problem across multiple points and from different perspectives.

Second, to create a complete picture of the problem situation, leaders must *respect the viewpoints of others.*

Third, problem-solving teams need *psychological safety* in order to experiment. We know that we still learn something if the experiment fails. It is important that people design and test solutions for learning, with learning being the goal. We are not proposing experiments that will negatively impact the customer; we are suggesting *small, fast, local experiments* that are contained and monitored to serve the customer better.

WHY ARE EFFECTIVE COMMUNICATIONS SO RARE?

Let's look at the insightful "communications laws" from Osmo A. Wiio, a Finnish professor of communication, who I (Jim) first learned about from an online course called Effective Communication Skills by Dalton Kehooe Ph.D., a senior scholar at York University in Toronto, Ontario.

(1) Communication usually fails, except by accident.
(2) If a message can be interpreted in several ways, it will be interpreted in a manner that maximizes damage.
(3) There is always someone who knows better than you what you meant by your message.

Although Wiio's laws are humorous, they do suggest that despite engaging in communications many times every day, we rarely communicate effectively. Effective communications happen when 1) we are understood by the other party, and 2) we are both happy with the interchange. It is a mutual connection of personal satisfaction.

More than anything, ineffective communication is caused by flawed assumptions that have developed into bad habits. The first flawed assumption is that we believe we see the world correctly and others do not. Our view is the best! If the other person does not understand our view of a situation, we assume it is their fault. Then, if the other person disagrees with our statement, we blame them for their ignorance.

The second flawed assumption is that we think we understand the intention of the other person. In 1970, Chris Argyris proposed the "Ladder of Inference" to describe how we move from a piece of observable information to invalid conclusions by believing we know the *thinking* of the other person. For example, Bill says, "I don't understand." Pete thinks Bill wasn't listening and says, "If you would listen, you might understand." Bill responds based on a false assumption about Pete's intention with, "You always make this a personal battle" ... etc. Each time both parties move up one more rung on the ladder making false conclusions about the situation. This "Ladder of Inference" process is a habit that makes effective and respectful communications totally impossible.

The facts are that we, humans, cannot see reality half of the time. Our sensory inputs are filtered and morphed to align with our assumptions. We tend to look for information that aligns with our beliefs and ignore evidence that conflicts with our beliefs. According to an article in 2012 in *Psychology Today*, we are very good at distorting reality. The natural filtering called confirmation bias is one of the most significant contributing factors to the way we interpret and share information. This is particularly a problem when we operate inside the Blanket Solutions paradigm. If we believe we have a solution, we tend to look for evidence that confirms the solution, and we ignore information that might suggest the solutions will not fix the problem. This bias makes us believe that we see the situation correctly, and others may not be able to see it as clearly. The default thinking is, "I am right, you are wrong." This distortion of reality is how we act in accordance with the unquestioned assumption of being a knower that we described in Chapter 5.

These ineffective communication behaviors are habits that have evolved and developed throughout our lifetime. We just need to practice new skills to overcome our deeply human difficulties.

THE NEUROSCIENCE OF TRUST AND DISTRUST

Trust and distrust emerge from different parts of the brain. Angelika Dimoka at Temple University describes this in her report, "What Does the Brain Tell Us about Trust and Distrust: Evidence from a Functional Neuroimaging Study." Trust is associated with higher brain activation from the pre-frontal cortex, the part of the brain responsible for cognitive skills. Distrust is associated with the amygdala, the emotional part of the brain, the part that is more automatically responsive to external stimuli. We get our emotions such as fear, defensiveness, anger, etc. from the amygdala. Distrust is automatic, but we can learn to overcome it through a conscious effort to have trust-building interactions.

According to a study by Paul J. Zak, a founding director of the Center for Neuroeconomics Studies at Clairmont Graduate University, higher levels of Oxytocin produce and predict trustworthiness. This conclusion is also documented in Judith Glaser's book, *Conversational Intelligence: How Great Leaders Build Trust and Get Extraordinary Results*, where she describes how leaders can increase Oxytocin levels and create higher levels of trust by learning the skill of dialogue. Unfortunately, we have observed very limited use of dialogue both in our interactions with companies and inside the Transformational Leadership Program.

The conclusion from all these studies of social systems and neuroscience is that leaders have a *profound* effect on building trust by practicing dialogue. Which brings us to the different types of communications.

THREE BASIC MODES OF COMMUNICATION

After reviewing many different models for classifying communications, we came up with this simplified approach, which identifies Dictate, Debate and Dialogue as the three basic communication modes.

Dictate: This type of communication generally goes only one way. The sender tells the receiver what he or she wants, and the receiver normally only asks questions for clarity. The receiver accepts the sender's command.

Debate: In this case, the sender is attempting to get the receiver(s) to accept his or her perspective. Both sides appear to be listening to each other but, ultimately, they are trying to change the thinking of the other side.

Dialogue: This type of communication requires deep respect for the other person's thinking, and all points of view are valued. It requires listening with empathy, being non-judgmental, and showing curiosity about what (and how) the other person is thinking. In order to listen intently, one needs to ask open-ended questions and shut off one's own thinking to understand the other. Then, if the respectful inquiry continues to go back and forth, the result can be something better than each individual perspective. This creates a wonderful synergy.

Of the three types of communication, only dialogue builds trust, demonstrates respect for the individual, and provides psychological safety. Dialogue, however, is a lesser developed skill. Most people lean toward either dictation or debate.

Dialogue and Problem Solving for Complexity

In 1996, famed theoretical physicist, David Bohm wrote a book titled *On Dialogue* where he offered a Theory of Dialogue where people could get together, have no agenda, listen to each other with no judgment, make no decisions, and then let the thinking emerge from the interchange. His view was that dialogue was prevalent in primitive societies but we have lost this art in our modern world. He believed that dialogue was the solution to changing the destructive nature of our current cultures.

TWO CRITICAL SKILLS FOR EFFECTIVE DIALOGUE: ACTIVE LISTENING AND HUMBLE INQUIRY

There are many resources for developing effective communications: from books and articles to custom approaches proposed by consulting firms. We have done the work of integrating the concepts from experts David Bohm, Judith Glaser, Amy Edmonson, Edgar Schein, Edwin Nevis, Sonya Nevis, and David Verble, to help you build these skills through deliberate practice. Two key communication skills that are important for you to learn are attentive listening and humble inquiry.

Attentive Listening

One of the key principles of attentive listening is to shut off your thinking (very hard to accomplish!) and listen attentively, with curiosity about the other person. The first step to become an attentive listener is to critique the kinds of questions we ask and statements we make, assessing how much of our thinking versus their thinking is going on in the conversation. Ask yourself, was that sentence a comment, statement, or suggestion, or was it a question? If it was a question, what kind of question was it:

- Open-ended
- Leading
- Based on what you are thinking
- Asking what the other person knows or thinks.?

Here is a table to help you understand the difference between typical closed-ended questions and open-ended questions.

Typical Closed Questions	More OPEN-ENDED Alternatives
"Did the power outage affect your computer?"	"**How** did the power outage affect your?"
Will you keep working until the project is done?	"**What** do you think it will take to catch up on the project?"
"Do you think the power will be back in the morning?"	"**When** do you think the power will be back on?"
"Do the computers need better surge protectors?"	"**What's** the best way to keep this from happening again?"
"Are you sure this will help"?	"**Why** do you think that will help?"

FIGURE 7.1
Closed and Open-Ended Questions Comparison.

A Simple but Powerful Shift

It is relatively easy to create practice sessions and evaluate the type of sentences you use in your communications with others.

As for the outcome of the practice session, you will want clarity on the following:

- Were you mostly Asking or Telling?
- Were your questions mostly Open-ended or Leading (yes or no)?
- Were your questions based mostly on what you were thinking or were you trying to learn about what the other person knew and was thinking? —Did you respect the other person's thinking?
- Did you mostly confirm things you already knew/thought or did you learn things you did not know?

Humble Inquiry

After a career of remarkable contributions in the field of organizational development, Edgar Schein wrote two simple but profoundly insightful books about making respectful connections between people. In 2011, he published "*Helping: How to Offer, Give, and Receive, Help.*" His second book "*Humble Inquiry: The Gentle Art of Asking Instead of Telling*" that came out in 2013, expands on the concepts of *Helping* and provides great guidance for leaders who want to become a role model for Dialogue.

Edgar Schein defines Humble Inquiry this way:

> Humble Inquiry is the fine art of drawing someone out, of asking questions to which you do not already know the answer, of building a relationship based on curiosity and interest in the other person … Ultimately the purpose of Humble Inquiry is to **build relationships that lead to trust** which, in turn, leads to better communication and collaboration.

To employ Humble Inquiry, we need to be genuinely curious about the other person's thinking and respect the other person for how they perceive the situation. We need to accept the fact that this person either knows more about the problem situation, or that what the other person knows can still significantly enhance our ability to grasp the situation. We need to shut down our judgment!

Here are some characteristics of Humble Inquiry:

- I maximize my curiosity about the other person
- I try to minimize my biases and assumptions
- I am sincere in my interest (people appreciate sincerity)
- My intent is to be openly curious and learn, help but not lead
- I listen to both the person and the words
- I try to create Equitability-in-the-Moment between us

Leaders seldom demonstrate humble inquiry with their employees. In the simulations inside Transformational Leadership, we not only validated that statement, but identified another characteristic that we call the hierarchy bias. With the hierarchy bias, respect flows in *one direction only, not both.* The subordinate listens carefully to the supervisor for the message, content, and intent, trying to understand the thinking behind the statement. The supervisor, on the contrary, does not necessarily listen to the subordinate as if their viewpoint is not as important. Here is an example.

In one simulation, after participants read all their emails, which contained bits and pieces of information about the company's business problems, the "CEO" called a meeting with his direct reports. They moved to a large table in the middle of an open room and began to share what each person had learned through the emails. In the meantime, the subordinates gathered in smaller groups discussing what they knew about the problems. After about an hour, one non-executive, a plant manager, wanted to talk with his boss who was at the executive table. Since there were no walls, plant manager knocked on an imaginary door trying to get his boss's attention. The boss turned around and waved his subordinate away making it clear he was not welcome in the elite group of executives.

It took us by surprise to see the hierarchy bias displayed in a simulation where leaders of equal status from different industries were gathering to think differently about their leadership style. They simply defaulted to the habit of underrating the knowledge of others. Needless to say, we saw evidence of the hierarchy bias in almost every simulation we have run so far.

Let's get back to what makes for a good question.

Schein suggests that there are three different "needs" for question. Either the question is about looking for solutions to a problem, or for facts to solve a problem, or finally, it's about finding out more about the other person. The only way to build trust is by engaging in learning more about the other person, not the problem situation.

Why is this so important? Most often, managers and leaders are uncomfortable with the idea of shutting off their thinking. Rightly so, they feel as if they have much to offer based on their extensive experience and feel a need to "give" this valuable experience to their employees and team members. It's only human. Our recommendation is to be the Humble Inquirer to *build the relationship first*. When you interject your own thinking prematurely, you own the problem and lose the opportunity to deploy problem responsibility to the subordinate. Tell your problem owner that you are not judging, but instead you respect their *thinking*. After this trusting connection is made, you can offer your experience and ask if this conversation helps you think differently about the problem situation.

Listening attentively and practicing humble inquiry help all of us as leaders honor the higher purpose of every individual, which is what enables us to build an extraordinary social system—a system that can respond to the fluid, chaotic world of change and that embraces the key characteristics of complex adaptive systems. Each person needs autonomy, respect, and the skill of communicating transparently with all others in the system. Each person needs to be able to pursue their higher purpose while contributing to the organizational needs. This may sound like a radical idea to you, but for us, we see this as a simple fact of human nature. People want to know that they matter and they want to make a meaningful contribution in the workplace.

I (Jim) recently attended a graduation ceremony where the keynote speaker was delivering a message to the graduates to "Find Their Higher Purpose." This is not a new concept. In fact, it's been around for a long time. Aristotle believed that all organisms have an end purpose. He used the Greek term, *Telos*, defined as purpose or end. He believed that all humans should continually move from imperfect to perfect to achieve their unique higher purpose of life. Leaders in most companies focus on the organizational purpose, not the purpose of the individuals. There is little evidence of leaders also knowing how to focus on supporting their people at moving toward their own higher purpose, their *Telos*.

This concept is best described by a story.

Performance Improvement by Honoring the Individual

Kathy, a young, bright, and focused graduate from a prestigious college, acquired a job in purchasing in a retail company that owned many luxury department stores. Kathy learned fast about her role as a buyer. She developed skills in how to interact with suppliers, select the right products, and negotiate pricing. She was recognized as a high potential employee and had a development career path that soon transferred her to be a department manager in a new store. This position was her first experience at being a manager.

Soon after she arrived at her new job in a different part of the country, Kathy was given an opportunity to hire a new sales team. She selected mostly young and inexperienced but eager to learn individuals and enthusiastically began to work with her new team. However, after about 6 months, she became very discouraged with her new assignment. Her sales numbers were not meeting company expectations, her team members were not responding to her orders, and she was ready to quit. Kathy was convinced she could not be a manager.

Then, she sought advice from experienced managers outside her company and listened carefully to their stories about the lessons they learned. She experimented with engaging her team in a process of creating the cycles of learning. Each team member accepted a challenge, experimented with it and each month reported on what they accomplished and learned. Then, they developed a plan for the next month. Everyone had a new challenge, and everyone had personal responsibility. The learning evolved but the most important thing that Kathy did was to honor each person by discussing their Telos, their purpose, and how she would help them grow to achieve their own desires. (These were the same skills needed to be better sales people). Kathy also went one step further. She convinced each sales representative to treat their customers the same way, i.e. to honor their being, not simply try to sell them products. She wanted her staff to create honest, trusting connections with customers and engage in discussion about what makes customers happy.

You might have guessed that the department performance began to break records. Customers walked away happy and the sales representatives felt the trust of their supervisor. Kathy demonstrated the kind of leadership that honors people, supports the development of each person's skills that help achieve their Telos, and the building of a trusting and respectful organization.

When you attend to the personal connections between people, you create a complex adaptive system of problem solvers. We believe the first order of business is for you, the leader, to practice building the skills of *attentive listening and humble inquiry.* You need to be the role model. You can structure the two different experiments offline, as a training session for those people you feel comfortable with. When you feel comfortable, begin modeling your new skills in front of your teams working on real problems. Explain that you are all learning new skills together.

To complete the three actions necessary for accomplishing a paradigm transformation, next we are going to discuss how to build a team, in which people at all levels are passionate about learning. This is the last "stone" in the foundation of an organization that continuously improves.

8

Accelerate Organizational Learning

> *"Learning organizations are where people continually expand their capacity to create the results they truly desire, where new and expansive patterns of thinking are nurtured, where collective aspiration is set free, and where people are continually learning how to learn together."*
>
> Peter Senge

FROM "LEARNING ORGANIZATIONS" TO "ORGANIZATIONAL LEARNING" TO AN "ORGANIZATION OF LEARNERS"

Developing learners is the final piece of the puzzle, the last of three actions needed for beginning the process of creating the problem solving for complexity culture. It's time for you to wrap your head around what we have learned about complex adaptive systems. It's time for you to think like a termite, the termite that created the first dirt ball for rebuilding the damaged termite mound.

We mentioned previously that culture change takes place from the bottom-up, not top-down. But it is so difficult for most of us to throw away all the beliefs we have developed about leadership where the leader is outside the system looking in, trying to influence the system. The important thing to remember is that, consistent with complex adaptive systems thinking, you are in the system, one of the individuals, and you are attempting to disturb the system through new, perhaps more intentional leadership actions. Or, as my (Jim') daughter Elizabeth once described it after observing me experiment with building my first koi pond:

> *The leader must attend to the balance of the eco-system, working to provide an environment where the people inside the system can thrive, allowing them to create the value for which they were hired. The leader is not well served to make forceful decisions that create large disturbances in the system, but rather engage small changes so as to allow the system to adapt to those changes more quickly. This is not only a sustainable model for growth, but an ethical model for the stakeholders of the business.*

What you learned in the previous two chapters, *the mindset for good problem solving* and *modeling attentive listening and humble inquiry,* are important parts of demonstrating your commitment. As we discussed in the Assumptions chapter, you need to model how to be a learner, not a knower so that each individual in your team may transition from being a knower to a learner as well. In this chapter, we discuss how to "make that first dirt ball." As a leader, you can begin the learning process by . . .

1. modeling being a learner, and
2. facilitating deep reflection sessions for the others to build their learner skills. These deep reflection sessions are a key part of PDCA learning cycles, described below.

There are many theories, books, and articles on building learning organizations, but Amy Edmonson makes a distinction between *learning organizations* and *organizational learning.* Building learning organizations tends to be about how complete organizations are able to change, while organizational learning focuses on individuals, attributing an organizational change to the changes in cognitive models. We want to build on Edmonson's model by refining the point on changing the mindset of each individual. Once again, we want to be specific about transitioning each individual from being a *knower to a learner.*

We can dig deeper into what it means to be a learner by looking into how Brian Hinken describes the behavior changes in "Confessions of a Recovering Knower." Moving from a knower to a learner is about making the following inner shifts:

- *From reacting to creating*
- *From compliance to commitment*
- *From protection to reflection*
- *From "my part" to "the whole"*
- *From debate to mutual learning*

The biggest difference between the two is that knowers restrict their own thinking! They stop short of clearly understanding the problem situation and often jump to what they believe is a solution. They don't dig deep enough. Knowers are not as humble and curious as learners. Learners continuously question the situation, looking for things they do not understand. They seek out different points of view believing that the system is complex, and they need others to discover good counter-measures to the problem.

CREATING LEARNERS IN COMPLEX ADAPTIVE SYSTEMS

The key characteristics of complex adaptive systems that relate to developing learners are:

1. Local nonlinear interactions resulting in self-organization
2. Solutions emerge from these local actions of the individuals as they work together looking for countermeasures
3. Small individual changes result in large organizational patterns
4. Feedback is used for ongoing correction moving performance toward the goal. Reacting to feedback keeps the system stable yet adaptable

For leaders to create change in a complex adaptive system, one must engage people to work together, allow self-organization, and ensure that the appropriate feedback measurements are in place for continuous adaptation. Learning takes place in complex adaptive systems as a result of the interactions between people solving problems together. The most effective way to learn as individuals in this system is to create continuous learning cycles focused on problem solving with deep reflection.

What should you expect from your team members? There are three different types of learning for people in your organization. First is that people should be learning new skills. Second, your people need to learn how to respond to problem gaps and feedback of the performance of the value stream they are engaged in. Third, people need to get in the habit of *learning how to learn*.

Learning new skills

- Learn how to identify problems, run experiments, and correct root causes
- Learn how to establish respectful connections to other team members

Learning about the Value Stream

- Learn how to identify problem gaps
- Learn how to reduce variation
- Learn how to create flow
- Learn how to provide corrective action feedback

Learning how to learn—become a learner vs. a knower

- Learn how to become passionate about PDCA learning
- Learn how to create daily, weekly, monthly plans
- Learn how to reflect on what worked/didn't work
- Learn how to be curious

The key to creating an organization where individuals are continuously learning depends on your ability to model the characteristics of a learner. Being humble, asking open-ended questions, honoring the individual, seeking to understand their thinking, and being curious is what accelerates learning. When you demonstrate all these learner characteristics *while facilitating intentional reflection sessions*, you become the catalyst for learning. People will follow your lead. Your passion for learning will be contagious.

Exposing problems takes leadership! It is natural to hide problems because we are fearful of being blamed by others. That is a part of our culture. As a leader, you can overcome that tendency by holding the assumption that failure is often caused by multiple interactions between people, systems, tools, processes, and policy. If the problem included all these interdependent contributing factors, then, individuals can be relieved of the embarrassment and fear of being singled out as the person who caused failure. Exposing problems and engaging people in the analysis is the key to learning.

DEEP REFLECTION THROUGH ACTION RESEARCH AND LEARNING CYCLES

"Action research" is the term for the process of uncovering solutions through progressive problem-solving activities. The outcome is intended to improve practices and address issues. Often performed by a group of participants, the process involves investigation through activity rather than theoretical response. This is called "participatory" action research.

Working to build the deliberate problem-solving framework along-side the methods of respectful communications we have discussed is one way to perform Action Research. When you add in the discipline of regular experiential learning cycles, you enable the learning to happen in the Action Research model. Learning cycles including creating plans, executing plans, learning from what worked and didn't work, and adjusting the plan for the next cycle are all key to Action Research. Action Research is a key part of creating and advancing learning cycles.

Remember, learning cycles have been around for a long time. Galileo contributed to cycles of learning by designing experiments to learn. Francis Bacon suggested that the generation of knowledge needed a planned struc-ture. And in the late 1800s, William James advanced learning cycles by suggesting the function of thought is to guide action. Structure provides room for creativity.

CONFUSION OVER LEARNING CYCLE MODELS

If there are many different models of learning cycles, which one should we use? Here 's a story

The end of the workshop is nearing, the energy in the room is high, and the participants are excited to share with their leaders what they learned about problem solving. The team is happy to tell their bosses that they uncovered some potential root causes of long-term perennial problems. Bob, the director of engineering, walks into the room with three other senior leaders. They greet the participants and sit down, waiting for the report-out. Sara, the manager of one of the engineering teams begins her report-out by describing the problem-solving process they learned. She explains the importance of grasping the situation, defining the problem, breaking down the problem, going to the workplace to see what is actually happening, selecting potential problem causes, and using PDCA to dig deeper into understanding the causes. Bob interrupts Sara, "What is PDCA?," he asks. She explains that it is a learning cycle based on learning through experience. He shouts back, "We don't use that here. We Use DMAIC."

POPULAR LEARNING CYCLE MODELS YOU SEE TODAY

DMAIC (Define–Measure–Analyze–Improve–Control)

DMAIC is part of the Six Sigma toolbox, the purpose of which is to provide a structured way to analyze problems and reduce variation in processes. The DMAIC learning cycle tends to be used by the internal specialist (i.e. Black Belt) as a part of their project management approach. It does not, however, emphasize people engagement and continuous improvement.

Cycle of Experience (Sensation–Awareness–Mobilization–Action–Contact–Withdrawal)

This cycle is part of Gestalt training where there is an emphasis on personal and group awareness using their energy as a way of managing through the cycle. It is especially effective for group alignment and agreement. Since this is oriented to social group process, it lacks the tools for the technical part of the problem to be addressed.

Kolb Learning Cycle (Concrete Experience–Reflective Observation–Abstract Conceptualization–Active Experimentation)

The focus in the Kolb learning cycle is to provide a framework for experiential learning. Kolb recognized that adults learn through experience. While his cycle has an emphasis on experimentation based on hypothesis, it does not help us understand how to select the right problems for problem solving.

OODA (Observe–Orient–Decide–Act)

OODA is the creation of Col. John Boyd, USAF. From my (Jim') reading, I've learned that he was the most effective air-to-air combat pilot in the USAF after he adopted this fast cycle of learning for personal survival. His emphasis is on overcoming our built-in beliefs and prejudices that prevent us from accurately assessing the current situation. Because speed in this model is important, OODA fails to incorporate reflection into the process. This model encourages recognition that you have an orientation that's causing a problem but does not help you change your habits because of the orientation.

LAMDA (Look–Ask–Model–Discuss–Act)

The development of LAMDA evolved from study of the Toyota Product/ Process Development by Alan Ward. Through this specialized learning cycle, Alan intended to create awareness that product development is primarily about knowledge creation and the need to create that knowledge quickly. LAMDA creates fast cycles of learning to enhance learning up-front, prior to the detailed design of the product development process. Because of this focus on knowledge of the technical design, it fails to build people capability through personal reflection and development.

PDCA (Plan–Do–Check–Adjust)

The development of PDCA has broad use as an iterative management method and the model for continuous improvement and learning. It has four distinct steps with reflection embedded in the Check and Adjust steps.

Although each of these special experiential learning cycles is useful in its own way, we find it beneficial to combine the basic problem-solving model with PDCA because of its simplicity. We understand that each organization may have different developmental needs. The benefit of PDCA and its simplicity is that any special needs can be integrated into the PDCA structure. For example, if product development needs to have greater in-depth investigation of technical solutions, that can be made a specific part of the PDCA learning cycles.

PDCA—THE CONCEPT IN PRACTICE

Some PDCA learning cycles begin with a project that has a specific expectation or goal in mind. Many times, in order to scope the project, you'll need a special activity to Grasp the Situation. For this reason, you'll see a 'fact-gathering funnel' that precedes the PDCA cycle of learning in Figure 8.1.

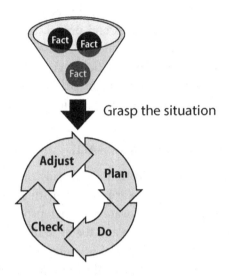

Grasp the situation

FIGURE 8.1
Understand What Is Actually Happening.

GRASP THE SITUATION

In the case of initiation of a project, you want to make a dedicated effort to understand the background, establish the current state, set the target, define who needs to be involved, establish overall goals and objectives, determine timeframe, and check with all stakeholders. Once all of this is done, work can begin on the project.

If, however, we look at PDCA as a continuous learning process, we need to think in terms of how and when people get together to learn. The first thing we need to establish is that PDCA is spelled incorrectly. It is actually CAP-D.

The more natural sequence of working with PDCA is to first check on *what is actually happening* now. How did our last plan work or not work? We need to check looking backwards. Then we need to A—adjust for the next plan. Finally, create a new short-term plan. Hence, the CAP sequence. These CAP reflection sessions can be the framework or agenda for regularly scheduled meetings. Then, there is a Do phase, when we execute the plan, between the CAP meetings. The process is shown in Figure 8.2.

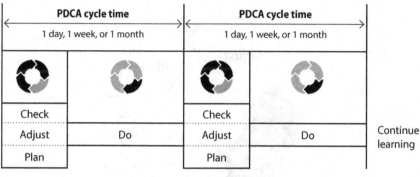

FIGURE 8.2
PDCA Learning Cycles with CAP-D Executions.

 START WITH C—CHECK

Problem-solving thinking starts with checking what is happening now and whether any actions we have taken are working or not working. In our practice, we have observed that the great majority of change initiatives are undertaken without a deep analysis of the process that is currently in place. When initiatives are added without knowing the current state, people create work-arounds and duplicate efforts that overcomplicate the process. You may add something that is already in play, or you may add something that you aren't ready for yet. "C" (Check) reminds us to stay in the moment and make incremental change. Check is needed to prevent a natural growth of complexity.

The Check phase requires us to take time to reflect on what is happening or what has happened in our experiment. The process of reflection should include the following questions:

- What was accomplished?
- Did we achieve our intended results?
- Did we follow the plan?
- What went well?
- What did not go well?
- What did we learn?

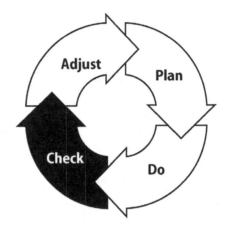

FIGURE 8.3
A Continuous Learning Process Starts with a Check.

An effective Check process for personal reflection can be used for understanding behaviors in the context of your organizational culture. This process includes the following steps:

- What Outcomes did we achieve, both planned and unplanned?
- What Actions did we take that resulted in the outcomes?
- What Conscious Thinking or hypothesis led to us taking these actions?
- What Unquestioned Assumptions led to us taking these actions?

We have found that a regular and continuous process of this reflection leads to personal experiential learning and practice around basic behavior modification. In other words, people will slow down, ask more open-ended questions, listen to each other, and build on each other's ideas.

WHY A?—ADJUST

Some organizations call the A-phase "Act" from the original Japanese version, but we prefer to call it "Adjust," because that is what we are doing to our plan based on the reflection of Check. After Check, we need to take advantage of what we have learned and make adjustments. Countermeasures are those actions needed to re-adjust and keep the plan on track. The

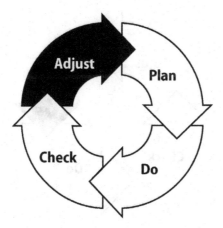

FIGURE 8.4
Use Learning from Your Reflection to Adjust.

adjustment should be the actions needed to correct the root cause of the existing problem situation. New actions should also address any unexpected outcomes and unanticipated consequences.

The key component to adjustment is focusing on what you have learned about the current state from reflection. Use of small, incremental adjustments is the most effective for true experimentation.

It is often helpful to include in this step the questions you answered from the last phase and new questions to get answered in this phase. Refer to the Knowledge Capture template in figure 8.8.

THE DISCIPLINE OF P—PLAN

Everything that results from the Check and Adjust phase is the Plan—to test your hypothesis. It is what you expect will happen if you apply the countermeasures.

A good plan has the following requirements:

- Goal—a description of an intended outcome and the purpose
- Responsibility—one person responsible for accomplishing the goal
- Target—the specific measurable condition to be achieved
- Features—description of the basic elements of what is needed to be changed

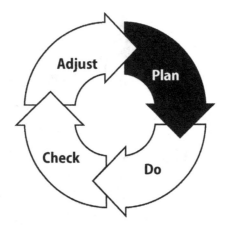

FIGURE 8.5
Plan Based on What You Learned from Check and Adjust.

- Support—the people who are needed to help the responsible person achieve the goal
- Action Steps, Responsibility, and Timing—each step in sequential order that is required to achieve the goal.

DO—MANY CYCLES OF PDCA

Implementation is another word for Do. Most companies spend much of their time doing things without the rest of the PDCA cycle. We "Do" actions in order to achieve a thorough understanding of our current problem situation including contributing problems and root causes. After we have done the hard work, we can suggest countermeasures and create our hypothesis, then we can "Do" actions to prove countermeasures and check our hypothesis. Many PDCA cycles are typically nested and running concurrently to achieve rapid results.

YOUR ROLE IN FACILITATING DEEP REFLECTION

When we ask the question "How would you describe your organization? Is it **PD**ca, or **P**dca, or p**D**ca, or **PDCA**?," the universal response is that there

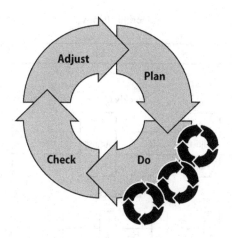

FIGURE 8.6
Implement Your Plan with Rapid Cycles of Learning.

is little reflection (Check and Adjust). Most people say their companies either practice Doing without Planning or focus on a lot of Planning with little Doing. Most organizations do very little Reflection, and yet this is what keeps implementation on track AND creates the foundation for learning. Leaders need to expect, model, and facilitate Reflection.

There are four specific reflection practices we recommend. The first practice is about how to create a structure to assure learning takes place at the right level at the right time and is consistent across the organization.

1. Aim to "Nest" PDCA Learning Cycles to Create Teams of Learners More Quickly

PDCA cycles should be embedded at different levels in the organization with different cycle times. At the value creator level, typically a fast *daily* learning cycle is appropriate for learning. Moving up one level, the team leaders or managers might consider weekly plans and PDCA cycles. Value-stream owners might pull together their teams on a monthly basis for reflection and creating a new plan.

Figure 8.7 shows how the three nested PDCA cycles relate to each other. At the highest level, the Value-Stream Owner is responsible for making sure the 30-day milestones are scheduled and that the Goal Owners and their team members are following a weekly PDCA cycle per the action plans. The Goal Owners are responsible for weekly PDCA cycles to implement their

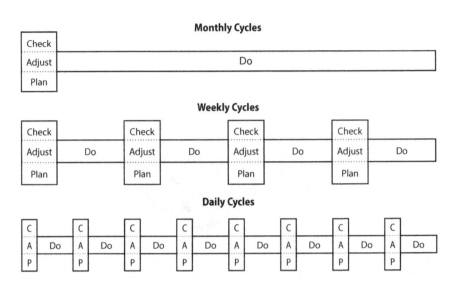

FIGURE 8.7
Nested PDCA Learning Cycles.

plans. At the lowest level, value creators are still learning more quickly, often daily, as they are seeking information or executing simple experiments.

Next, organizations struggle at keeping a knowledge base so that they can grow from what they already have learned rather than re-learning in multiple places. Here is a simple way to capture learning and guide the learning process to accelerate the rate of learning.

2. Use "Knowledge Capture Templates" to Accelerate Individual and Team Learning

What we know	How we know it
What we need to know *(Questions)*	Fastest way to get answers *(Actions)*

FIGURE 8.8
Knowledge Capture Template.

For each learning cycle, encourage the team members to learn quickly. You can support and accelerate this learning process by using a knowledge capture template. The key to solving problems is to be clear on what you know and don't know, what you need to learn, and how to get the fastest answer to the questions. The template below keeps your team focused on what is important as you learn quickly.

Figure 8.8 introduces the knowledge capture template that is intended to keep the focus on learning. Using the template is a way to create alignment, find points of agreement, and focus on learning. It also provides a way to keep visible what is known for potential communication to other teams. The direct output from this process is a set of actions that need to be prioritized to be accomplished the next week. You can add these action items to the next chart so you have a trackable action list to be followed daily.

Most companies focus on task completion wherein the leader asks the team member, "Did you complete your tasks?" The team member's aim then is to answer yes, get an item checked off the list, and just move on to avoid embarrassment. In order to create an organization of learners, the leader needs to change the review process from a checklist process to a deep reflection process (Check and Adjust). Below is a process we suggest you use to encourage deep reflection. It's your job to facilitate these reflection sessions and encourage open dialogue.

3. Create a Standard Process for Team Reflection

Inside PDCA cycles, reflect on what worked, what didn't work, and what was learned so that you and your team can create a new plan for the next learning cycle. The fastest way to build the mindset of a learner is to facilitate these reflection sessions. Again, the PDCA cycle is really structured CAP-D. The meeting you facilitate is *Check–Act–Plan*. The meeting starts with an analysis of what was done in the cycle timeframe by each team so that you can develop a new plan.

Here is a typical agenda for a Reflection Session:

- Share Accomplishments (**Check**)

- ○ Participants sit across a table and tell each other what they have accomplished since the last Reflection Session
- ○ Discussion is around what was accomplished, not what did not get done or what went wrong (Appreciative Inquiry)

- Performance to Plan (**Check**)

  - ○ Each team reviews the plan created the last time
  - ○ Each team assesses what parts of the plan were executed vs. not executed. This is normally captured by marking up the plan.

- Evaluation and Learning (**Check**)

  - ○ Capture what worked
  - ○ Capture what didn't work
  - ○ Capture what was learned

- Countermeasures and Questions (**Adjust**)

  - ○ Capture high-level expectations for next plan
  - ○ Capture what are the countermeasures for the items that did not work
  - ○ Develop a list of questions to be answered this time

- Create a new plan for this cycle (**Plan**)

  - ○ Goal and person responsible
  - ○ Targets and measurement
  - ○ Features and questions to answer
  - ○ Support team
  - ○ Actions—Responsibilities—Due Dates

Leaders who facilitate this reflection process will see the organization move toward better problem solving, better communication, and deeper learning that includes layers of self-reflection. Learning about value-stream performance is one level of learning; real culture change requires multiple levels of learning, all happening simultaneously. As you grow the processes for learning throughout your organization, you might facilitate a reflection session with the managers you have engaged to look for evidence of moving toward the Problem Solving for Complexity paradigm.

4. Reflect on How the Transition to the New Paradigm is Going

You may notice that the kind of reflection we're advocating here is not at all the same as what you see in many assessment tools out there today. For example, the Shingo Prize Model, broadly used to assess the effectiveness of Lean transformations, is clearly connected to the Blanket Solutions paradigm because it measures Lean based on the implementation of Lean tools as solutions. In other words, "You are a Lean organization if you take these actions and use these tools." Reflection inside the Problem Solving for Complexity paradigm is different in that it requires an honest look at the current condition, asks what should be the next near-term target, and decides what countermeasures (experiments) can move you toward the next target. In addition, this higher level reflection should not be as detailed as most assessment tools out there today, but instead, stay at a higher level looking at assumptions that drive behavior. This type of high-level reflection, not "assessment," is ongoing and should be done by leaders on a regular basis to assess how assumptions are changing (or not changing) over time. We suggest that senior leaders gather quarterly to perform such reflection sessions using the model we covered in Figure 5.1. In this reflection session, leaders can evaluate any changes to assumptions based on their observation of how teams work together at Problem Solving for Complexity. They can create countermeasures based on what they believe process gaps are in evolving from one paradigm to the other.

Building the discipline of learning cycles is the key to continuous learning and enabling individuals to move from being knowers to becoming learners. Your role is not to drive the process, but to embed yourself in the continuous learning by facilitating reflection sessions. You can demonstrate your curiosity and passion for learning in these sessions. You will see people grow and your organization's problem-solving capabilities adapt to the fast-changing challenges you want to be able to overcome.

In Part 4, Actualization, we give you a guide for thinking about exactly this kind of personal leadership development. The first chapter is about how you can practice new skills for leading the paradigm shift . . . because, again, a good leader creates the conditions for organizational health and improved performance. We'll talk more about small, impactful experiments that you can run to focus on your personal growth as a leader while helping along organizational learning. Remember, this co-development method is always done in the context of solving business problems. In Chapter 10, we share the stories of several leaders who embrace the concepts we cover in this book. In their own words, they describe what it's been like to learn to lead differently in order to achieve meaningful culture change in their organizations. These are people who inspire us in our work as leaders and thinkers, and we hope they inspire you as well.

Part 4

Actualization

How to Step Into Your Potential as a Leader

Medice, cura te ipsum. Translated from Latin, this proverb means "Physician, heal yourself." In this book, we dedicated many pages to your leadership role in moving your organization to the Problem Solving for Complexity paradigm. But what about *you*?

Do *you* have the knowledge and skills to lead a complex adaptive system, your company/division/team, through change? Do you have what it takes to help your people sustain the momentum gained during initial improvement efforts and set the organization on a path for a long-lasting success and prosperity? If you happened to develop as a leader inside your current paradigm, most likely some of your skills and habits need to change.

We are aware that your desire and ability to learn may be affected by several factors, first and foremost, your own assumptions. As we discussed in the chapter on leadership assumptions, our society, or what we refer to as "Western culture," supports and rewards knowers. The grooming starts on day one in the kindergarten, and by the time a person is promoted to senior leadership ranks, the habit is fully formed: to excel, one needs to look confident and knowledgeable (even when it may not be the case), and always be ready to produce a solution to any problem... as quickly as possible! Being humble, self-reflective, and eager to continuously improve and learn are not the traits that come to mind right away when we think about leaders.

And, of course, time is always an issue. Leaders are busy. Senior leaders are insanely busy. Where should one get the time to squeeze learning into a never-ending sequence of meetings, conference calls, presentations, speaking engagements, reviews, off-sites, and networking? To say nothing about e-mail ...

We don't promise it's going to be easy. But the benefits will be astounding, and not just for you but for everyone around you. We've said it before and, at the risk of boring you with repetition, we'll say it again: people copy leaders! Your readiness to admit you may not have a solution to every problem, your desire to actualize your personal transformation, and your dedication to learning will inspire everybody around you to learn and improve. By launching your personal transformation, you will initiate the formation of an organization of learners. We wrote this Part to help you create the structure and process for your personal learning journey.

Chapter 9, *Start with Yourself*, puts your development into the context of an organizational transformation. In it, we discuss how you can identify critical skills needed for you to be able to provide maximum support to your company's change effort, and introduce a skill-building process that will help you accelerate your learning.

Chapter 10, *Stories of Leadership Transformations*, contains a collection of stories written by and/or about leaders who have experienced an a-ha moment, realized the need to change and embarked on the never-ending journey of personal learning. We know each of these leaders and admire their focus on self-actualization and the hard work they put into personal improvement and growth.

Medice, cura te ipsum: Physician, heal yourself!

9

Start with Yourself

"Yesterday I was clever, so I wanted to change the world. Today I am wise, so I am changing myself."

Jalaluddin Mevlana Rumi

YOUR SKILL DEVELOPMENT IN THE CONTEXT OF ORGANIZATIONAL TRANSFORMATION

It would be nice to have the luxury of endless time to work on your skills first and then, once you feel ready, initiate your organization's paradigm transformation. It may happen after you have led a number of change efforts and run lots of experiments that helped you expand your skill "portfolio." But if this is your very first attempt at steering your company away from the Blanket Solutions paradigm while helping it build the muscle for Problem Solving for Complexity, you have no other way but to learn together with your team as your team takes a stab at solving value-stream problems.

The learning path will consist of many learning cycles and many sets of experiments, with both you and your people going through quick cycles of PDCA, taking small steps toward your target. The success of this exercise depends on your ability to take off your *knower* hat and become a *learner*. It will require you to admit to your team that you are going to learn together with and alongside them. Moreover, you may need to ask them for help by giving you a timely constructive feedback on your learning progress. It may feel uncomfortable at first, but once you see how much your team members appreciate your openness and humility—and how eager they are to support your efforts to build new skills—you will gradually begin to shape yourself into the learner.

MASTERING THE ART OF HUMBLE INQUIRY WHILE SOLVING A PTOI PROBLEM

A couple of years ago I (Olga) got to coach a senior leader who participated in his company's executive development program. One of the program blocks was dedicated to the work on a problem from each participant's operation. An interesting twist was that the participants weren't expected to solve the problem on their own. They needed to form a team and lead it through the problem-solving process. The problem that my executive coachee selected for this project was about a wide range in performance on his sales team, with a variance in volume of over several hundred thousand dollars. This variation directly affected the company's PTOI (pretax operating income) and its potential for business growth.

On day one of the project, my coachee expressly stated that he wanted to help the team as much as possible . . . which, in his case, meant giving them every solution he could come up with. He completely dominated the first two reflection sessions when the team was sharing what they had learned about the current state of the problem. As an industry and company veteran, he knew the business inside out and could produce all kinds of data followed by immediate conclusions. After the second session, in our one-on-one reflection, I asked him to assess a progress in building problem-solving capabilities by his team members. He seemed puzzled by the question and initially began to talk about the progress they made in solving the problem. I explained that it wasn't what I wanted to know. The purpose of my question was to make him realize that until that moment, his only goal was to solve the problem . . . quickly! And he was way too ready to provide the solution. Was this actually helpful for the long-term development of his team?

By the end of our reflection, he reset his priorities and decided to shift his focus from the solution/result to the process, helping his team improve their problem-solving capabilities. We discussed how humble inquiry can help him stop inserting his own thinking into the team's work. We talked about how he might practice asking open-ended questions about the current state of their problem. The next team meeting started with my coachee sharing his insights, saying that he was going to practice working differently. He asked them to tell him, in the moment, when he would bounce back to his habit of telling rather than asking. His team happily agreed to help him.

The next few weeks were filled with intensive learning as my coachee was mastering the art of humble inquiry. Initially, team members were having a lot of fun asking him to stop every time he was beginning to tell them what he thought needed to be done. Soon though, as he got better at resisting "to tell," they noticed how much they appreciated his questions. Every time team members had a new insight provoked by one of my coachee's good questions, we celebrated. It didn't take long for the whole team to shift to the questioning mode. They began to listen much more carefully to each other. As a result of this work, the team identified the root causes of the problem they were working on and tested countermeasures to help bridge the gap in the sales team's performance. Most importantly, the leader and the team developed an appreciation for a respectful communication style and its impact on everyone's ability to solve problems.

In this case, the leader identified a gap in his skills after the business problem had been identified. We encourage you, however, to think about a skill or skills that you want to improve at the same time as you select a business problem to address. Develop a detailed plan for what, when, where, and how you are going to practice. Otherwise you risk that the reasons that we discussed earlier will distract you from learning.

To help you initiate and structure your learning, we will use a template that we created for the participants of the Transformational Leadership Program. It is very similar to an A3 storyboard that Lean practitioners use to capture their problem-solving process.

An A3 is an 11"×17" piece of paper used as a storyboard for describing the problem-solving thinking that led the creator to propose certain actions to address an organizational or operational performance issue or need to improve performance capability. Most importantly, A3 is a tool that supports coaching, management, and communication practice. If you want to learn more about the A3 process, we recommend the 2009 MIT Sloan Management Review article "Toyota's Secret: The A3 Report" by John Shook and the book Managing to Learn: Using the A3 Management Process, also by John Shook.

The main difference between this template and a traditional A3 document is that the latter usually focuses on one problem, whereas in our case, we suggest that you capture your work on a business problem along with your personal development story.

Title: *Business problem that needs to be solved*

BACKGROUND	
What needs to be improved and why? (Something I own or influence)	
In the business:	In myself in order to improve the business:
CURRENT STATE	
What are the facts of the problem / situation?	
In the business:	In regard to my lesser-developed skills:
PROBLEM STATEMENT (one concise sentence)	
What is the gap that needs to be closed?	
In the business:	In myself in order to improve the business:
GOALS / EXPECTED OUTCOMES	
How much of the gap needs to be closed?	
In the business:	In myself in order to improve the business:
CAUSE ANALYSIS	
What systemic issues caused the gap?	*What assumptions and habits caused the gap?*
In the business:	In myself in order to improve the business:

FIGURE 9.1

A3 Storyboard Template.

Owner:

PROPOSED COUNTERMEASURES	
What experiments will I try?	
In the business:	To improve my lesser-developed skills:

PLAN	
What steps will I take to make improvements and when?	
What and how will I practice?	
In the business:	To improve my lesser-developed skills:

FOLLOW-UP	
How will I know if there is improvement?	
How will I know if things go off plan?	
What is my process for ongoing reflection / PDCA?	
In the business:	In myself in order to improve the business:

FIGURE 9.1
(Continued)

THE FIRST AND MOST IMPORTANT QUESTION: WHAT IS THE PROBLEM?

The very first question to ask is what needs to be improved and why, both in the business and in yourself in order to improve the business. In other words, you need to put a value-stream problem you believe needs to be addressed into the context of organizational priorities. And you want to put your personal skill gap into the context of that business problem.

We predict that you'll discover you have multiple skill gaps that need to be closed. So what do you do? Do you try to attack them all? Don't spread yourself too thin trying to build too many new capabilities at once. Select one that, when improved, will allow you to be most helpful to your team in solving this particular business problem. Just make sure that the skill you select is one of your lesser developed skills.

You may ask why you need to practice lesser developed skills.

We all have greater developed and lesser developed skills. When we work on developing our capabilities, we naturally focus on skills that are already in a good shape. Why? Because System Two in our brain (revisit Chapter 4 if needed!) takes us down the path of least resistance, just like it steers us toward blanket solutions when we deal with problems. It is easier to work on greater developed skills because practicing them takes less effort.

Attempting to help your organization transform its current dominant paradigm requires you to stop focusing on the skills that you built within your existing paradigm and begin to work on skills that are critical to accomplishing a paradigm shift, which, most likely, you developed to a lesser degree or not at all.

The story below has nothing to do with the world of business. It is, however, a good illustration of the benefits of focusing on lesser developed skills.

Even if you don't play or watch tennis, most likely you know about Roger Federer. He has won unprecedented 20 Major titles and at the age of 38 seems to be playing his best tennis ever. You may not know though that between 2012 and 2017, Federer went through a 5-year Grand Slam title drought. It looked like the Federer era was over when he suddenly came back setting new records, challenging existing sports longevity standards, and making fans and experts gasp in admiration asking how it was even possible.

What happened? What did Roger do to not only get back to the top but become an even better player than he was in his twenties?

For years, Roger amazed the tennis world with his forehand. It was a weapon that he used often and with great results. Seeing him run around the ball to hit an inside-out forehand winner was a treat. His backhand, however, had always been a liability, which is why he often resorted to a defensive slice instead of hitting an offensive topspin. For some time, his strengths compensated this weakness. Until a lefty Rafael Nadal began to punish him, match after match, pounding heavy topspin forehands to Roger's backhand and forcing Federer to make mistakes. When it became obvious that this strategy worked, other players followed suit. And, as the number of tournaments Federer entered but didn't win grew, the media started betting on his retirement date.

Then, in 2014, Federer switched to a bigger racquet that helped him better connect with a ball and hit better topspin backhand shots. This racquet was tougher to control which is why Roger spent many hours on the court practicing backhand returns. "I think the backhand has gotten better because I have been able to put in so many hours onto the racquet now," he told reporters in one of his press conferences a couple of years later. "I think all my coaches through my career have told me to go more for the backhand. Maybe deep down I didn't believe I had it in the most important moments. But I think that's changing little by little, which I'm very happy about."

Roger Federer became an outstanding tennis player by using and tirelessly improving his major strength, the forehand. But what made him a legend, perhaps the greatest player of all time, was his effort to improve his weaker, lesser developed backhand.

The (Macro) PDCA of Your Own Development

Just as you follow PDCA cycles when you work on business problems, you can use this method to close your personal skill gaps. We refer to it here as the *"macro PDCA"* because inside this process, you will run lots of quick experiments (*micro PDCA cycles*) to make sure you are building the right skill the right way.

Here are the key steps you will need to take in your macro PDCA cycle.

Understand Your Competency Gap

When you work on a business problem, you need to have a solid grasp of the problem situation. It is no different when it comes to competency building: it starts with understanding the size and the nature of your skill gap. To do this, look around and identify some folks who, in your opinion, have a high level of mastery of this new skill and compare your own skills to theirs. You can also ask your peers or direct reports to give you feedback when they observe you attempting to demonstrate a new skill you are working on. Finally, find a coach and ask him/her to support you through your skill-building process, starting with the initial assessment of your competency level. Be prepared to approach this exercise with a great deal of humility. As an accomplished leader, we

BACKGROUND	
What needs to be improved and why? (Something I own or influence)	
In the business:	In myself in order to improve the business:
CURRENT STATE	
What are the facts of the problem / situation?	
In the business:	In regard to my lesser-developed skills:
PROBLEM STATEMENT (one concise sentence)	
Describe the gap that needs to be closed	
In the business:	In myself in order to improve the business:

FIGURE 9.2
Understand the Gap.

imagine you are used to being praised for your talents and achievements. Asking people to observe how you do something you are not 100% great at may be a humbling experience. (This is when it helps to remember Roger Federer!)

Set the Target

The more specific you are about your target, the better. Try to visualize (or even draw!) what it will look like when you master the desired skill. Bring positive emotions into your description or drawing. The description of your target condition should be inspiring enough to get you out of bed every morning and make you want to start practicing right away. Our brain reacts to both positive and negative triggers, but research shows that positive emotions help make learning more effective.

For example, if you want to get better at coaching with humble inquiry, you can say that your goal is to ask open-ended questions in coaching conversations with your team members and resist from imposing your solutions on them. The purpose for doing this is to help your coachees' refine their thinking about problems and support the development of their problem-solving capabilities. This is a clear and specific target, and you'll be fine using it just as is. Or you can take it to the next level by creating the image of what achieving this goal will look like: "Every time I ask a question, I see a spark of insight in my coachee's eyes". When you phrase it this way, it may not meet all the criteria of a SMART goal but it makes you smile, doesn't it? That's because you can envision how great it will feel when your question will help a coachee

GOALS / EXPECTED OUTCOMES	
How much of the gap needs to be closed?	
In the business:	In myself in order to improve the business:

FIGURE 9.3
Set Gap-Closing Targets.

create a new neural connection and learn something new about the problem and themselves. Folks at the NeuroLeadership Institute founded by David Rock refer to this process as "shining" suggesting that it creates an emotional attachment and commitment to the goals.

Understand the Assumptions that Caused the Gap

There is something else that *only you* can do to better understand the current state of your competency gap: the analysis of your thinking and assumptions that, so far, have prevented you from developing this new particular skill.

It is not enough to admit that you are not great at defining problems at the point of delivery to the customer; or that you don't spend enough time at the workplace supporting the development of your team's problem-solving capabilities; or that you find asking instead of telling to be a challenge, etc. To close a skill gap, you need to understand what caused it. So go ahead and do some soul searching! To make this easier, think about specific examples/situations when you failed to demonstrate the skill in question and ask yourself what triggered it. Your assumptions are the root causes of your skill gaps so, just like it is critical to identify root causes when you solve value-stream problems, it is equally important to dig deep enough to understand causality behind your skill deficiencies.

CAUSE ANALYSIS	
What systemic issues caused the gap?	*What assumptions and habits caused the gap?*
In the business:	In myself in order to improve the business:

FIGURE 9.4
Examine Causality.

Design Experiments and Create Your Practice Plan

Practicing a skill is a PDCA-based cyclical process based on rapid experimentation, with every practice round helping you get closer to

PROPOSED COUNTERMEASURES	
What experiments will I try?	
In the business:	To improve my lesser-developed skills:

PLAN	
What steps will I take to make improvements and when? *What and how will I practice?*	
In the business:	To improve my lesser-developed skills:

FIGURE 9.5
Plan for Practice.

your target. To make sure you are achieving expected results, your plan needs to include answers to the "what," "where," "when," and "who" questions relative to the experiments you want to run.

WHAT Are You Going to Practice?

Define very specific actions that you will perform as part of your practice cycle. It is not enough to say, "I am going to practice coaching with humble inquiry." Instead, consider articulating specific details of your practice. For example, "I am going to ask open-ended questions about the current state of a problem that Person X is working on to ensure he/she has a good grasp of the problem situation."

WHERE Will You Practice?

Start with a selection of your practice area, i.e. situations where you will feel safe and comfortable to try something new. A Board meeting may not be the best place to practice humble inquiry. Make sure the area you select will provide an opportunity to practice regularly (ideally daily, or at least several times a week).

WHEN Will You Practice?

Again, be as specific as possible. If you have repeated events in your calendar that will allow you to try a new skill, mark them! If not, put your practice cycles on the calendar and make sure you don't double-book those slots.

WHO Is Going to Help You?

Find a "practice buddy," someone you trust and enjoy working with who can observe you practice a new skill and give you an honest feedback, maybe with some humor, too.

A SIDE NOTE ON THE NEUROSCIENCE OF LEARNING

All right, you have defined your gap, you understand what causes it, you've designed some experiments to run, and you've created a practice plan. Excellent. Now it's time to put your practice into practice!

Recent discoveries in neuroscience have taught us a great deal about capability building by demonstrating the connection between the mechanics of skill development and the processes that take place in the brain. (At the end of the book, we list additional books by Daniel Coyle, Daniel Kahneman, and David Rock on the subject of brain-based learning.)

The human brain contains about 100 billion neurons. Every time we learn something new, we create a new neural connection in the brain. To convert new knowledge into skill, we need to practice. Every time we practice, a matter called myelin wraps around the circuit helping increase the strength, speed, and accuracy of this signal. The more we fire the same circuit, the more myelin grows around it. And the thicker the myelin layer is, the more automated our thoughts and movements become.

Scientists had known about myelin for a long time before they discovered its role in skill building. Maybe you heard about it, too. It was usually referred to as "white matter." For a long time, there was no clarity around what it was responsible for, so it was considered a passive tissue. That is, until experiments allowed scientists to uncover the role that white matter plays in learning and skill development. Composed of myelinated axons or nerve fibers, white matter connects various gray matter areas and carries nerve impulses between neurons. Myelin wraps around axons and acts as an insulator helping increase the speed of transmission of all nerve signals. Electric signals travel through neural circuits with a lightning-fast speed, which explains why learning something new on *a cognitive level* usually doesn't take a long time. When we receive new information, the brain organizes neurons to create a new circuit to process it and *voila!* we "get it."

But this is not so with skill development. *It just takes time to progress from a conceptual comprehension of a new idea to actually being able to do something about it.* The reason for the delay is myelin! It takes time for it to grow. And it only grows when we intentionally fire neural circuits ... in other words, when we practice. Stop practicing, and your brain may eventually "forget" you even built this new circuit. Keep firing the circuit, and the thickening layer of myelin will make sure you get progressively better at executing the new skill. Daniel Coyle puts it this way: "Skill is myelin insulation that wraps neural circuits and that grows according to new signals." When we learn something new and work to turn this new knowledge into a new capability, we actually make changes to our brain, increasing the number of neural circuits and the layer of myelin wrapped around them.

WHY CAN SKILL BUILDING BE SO FRUSTRATING?

Three cheers for myelin and all of us finally understanding how myelin works, but you can still spend hours, days, months and, sometimes, years, working on a skill without achieving your desired level of competency. What gives? More often than not, it happens because you didn't practice right. It takes a special type of practice to build lesser developed skills and make them "stick." It involves more than just repeating an action or trying a behavior many times. In fact, simple repetition may lead you in a wrong direction.

Continuing on a tennis theme, in my club, I (Olga) often see an older gentleman whose dedication to practice is admirable. He is on the court almost every day, with a basket of balls, hitting serves. Hundreds of them. Toss, swing, hit ... Toss, swing, hit ... About one third of balls makes it into the service area, the rest either hit the net or go out. It is not a great percentage and, despite all the time and effort that this gentleman puts into his practice, the accuracy of his serve doesn't seem to be improving. You must have already guessed what the issue here is ... his technique is wrong. And by repeating the same motion over and over he reinforces bad habits. Myelin wraps around a circuit that actually shouldn't exist in the first place.

There is a better way to practice.

A BETTER WAY TO PRACTICE: RAPID LEARNING EXPERIMENTS (MICRO PDCA) TO BUILD YOUR LESSER DEVELOPED SKILLS

PDCA-based practice is a cyclical progression through four steps:

1. Set the target
2. Practice (one round)
3. Pause and reflect
4. Make adjustments as needed

Repeat the cycle until you achieve your target level of proficiency.

We have already discussed the macro PDCA cycle, during which you create a high-level practice plan, so let's dive right into the practice itself or the "DO" step of your macro PDCA. The key idea here is experimentation. It is important to think about this step as a *number of micro PDCA cycles*, each cycle serving as a rapid learning experiment, with reflection and adjustment immediately following each of your attempts at practicing a new skill.

Once you begin to practice, go through one round, then pause and reflect on your experiment. If you are working with a practice buddy, get their feedback, reflect more, and then decide which adjustments you need to introduce in your next practice. You want to make sure that myelin wraps around the right new circuit!

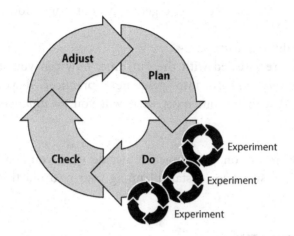

FIGURE 9.6
Macro and Micro PDCA Cycles.

WE NEVER GET TIRED OF SAYING IT: REFLECTION IS KEY

In previous chapters, we discussed the enormous value of reflection in helping accelerate learning across your organization. Developing the habit to reflect on the effectiveness of your personal practice is equally vital!

Reflection is the most important (and the least practiced) step of PDCA. In today's fast-paced world, we tend to focus on "planning" and "doing," rarely clearing our schedules to reflect on the effectiveness of these two steps. In fact, most leaders we talk with say that they don't have time to plan, so they move directly from an idea to execution. When we talk to them about reflection, we usually get stares and hear something like, "Are you kidding?! We don't have time to reflect."

David Fleming famously said, *"Forward movement is not helpful if what is needed is a change of direction."* If we spend all of our time moving back and forth between "plan" and "do," never pausing to reflect on the effectiveness of our plans and actions, how will we know we are moving in the right direction?

Here is a simple, yet effective approach to personal reflection.

- Start with an *outcome*: What came out of your practice round? Are you satisfied with it?

- What *action* did you take to get to this outcome? How do you feel about it?
- What did you *learn*?
- If you are satisfied with the outcome, how can you incorporate the *lessons learned* into your next practice? If you are not satisfied with the outcome, what will you *do differently* in your next practice?

Once you reflect on your practice, decide what you want to adjust and go back to step one ... start planning your next practice round.

OVERCOMING THE BIGGEST CHALLENGE TO YOUR LEARNING

You guessed it. It's you.

None of what we've shared with you so far about the approach to improving your lesser developed skills, PDCA-based practice, the importance of reflection, etc. is relevant if your own habits get in the way of your learning. And you already know that your habits can detract from others' ability to build new skills. Here are some habits that leaders need to overcome to allow for learning to take place:

Persistent Noisy Thoughts

We self-talk all the time replaying what happened yesterday, playing out our next day and criticizing others. Experts believe we have somewhere between 60,000 and 80,000 thoughts per day, most about the past or the future, repeated over and over again, all resulting in little value. All this mental chatter prevents us from focusing on what is important ... learning.

Constant Interruptions

We have seen this scenario in almost every workshop we've done where senior leaders were present. The most senior person either arrives late or steps out to take a call or leaves in the middle of the workshop to go to a "more important" meeting. These actions result in lost focus and disruption of learning for the whole group. Moreover, the people who remain in the room feel put down because the leader has just communicated to them that they are lower in the hierarchy, hence less important.

Quick Judgment

We have all been trained to make quick decisions. We usually do this based on some new observation, add some experience or intuition into the mix, and then either categorize someone or take a reactive (not responsive) new action. We judge in the moment without the benefit of the context or hearing the views of others. This habit prevents us from effectively listening and being open to new ideas. We are just too busy judging.

To become more effective in your own learning and to create an environment that supports the learning of others, try to build these new habits:

Present Moment Awareness

Shut off the self-talk and turn off the noise. Stay in the present moment. Watch, listen, and pay attention to what is happening now. Listen to others with the intent to understand their thinking. In a group setting, observe how others are listening, pay attention to who is talking/not talking, and look for opportunities to capture and share learning.

Taking in the Goodness

Instead of judging, simply look for the good things that are happening. Even when things don't go the way you may want them to go, honor the opportunity to learn from the situation.

Appreciating the Now

In the learning environment, look for the energy created by the people. Do not stop the flow and growth of energy in the room by interjecting your ideas or thoughts. Encourage and reinforce their shared thinking. Keep focused on energy, not the content of the discussion.

THE UNPARALLELED JOY OF LEARNING

For many of us, every time we learn something new, we experience the joy of suddenly "getting it." It feels wonderful, it feels motivating, and it makes us want to continue learning. Remember Archimedes' "Eureka!" moment when he discovered what is now known as the Archimedes principle?

Let's be clear. We don't advocate that you repeat his naked run through astonished Syracuse every time you learn or achieve something new. We just want you to welcome the joy of learning, the energy you get from it, and the unstoppable desire to keep improving when you fire new circuits in your brain.

What is truly awesome about this feeling is that it will not wear off over time. Kids and adults feel equally overjoyed when they experience a Eureka moment. It's the winter of 2019 when I (Olga) am writing this. Just a few days ago, New England Patriots won their ninth AFC Championship Game, and 41-year-old QB Tom Brady celebrated the victory with more excitement than when he led the Pats to win his first Lamar Hunt Trophy in 2001, 18 years ago. It wasn't just about winning the championship; he was happy that he and the team were able to achieve yet another height as a result of collaborative learning and focused dedication and practice.

FIGURE 9.7
A Joyful Eureka Moment.

We encourage you to capture the moments when you suddenly experience excitement because you just attempted to try something new and it worked. Treasure these moments. Share them with others. Invite your team members to join you in the kind of learning that will enrich you all intellectually and emotionally as you work together to transform your organization and solve real problems that make a difference.

10

Stories of Leadership Transformations

> *A leader is best when people barely know he exists, when his work is done, his aim fulfilled, they will say: we did it ourselves.*
>
> Lao Tzu

We have had the privilege to know and work with some remarkable people, leaders who have stepped out of their comfort zones to create energetic organizations and achieve extraordinary success. These leaders at one point had an awakening, the big a-ha moment wherein they realized they had to start changing themselves.

Here are a few of their stories.

TAKING MY LEADERSHIP TO A HIGHER LEVEL

By Mike Emery

With over 20 years of management experience, I had forgotten what it felt like to be in a position where I truly had no idea what to do. So standing in front of about 40 people—people who at the time experienced their work as chaos and were looking at me for leadership to make it better— was a rude surprise. I didn't know how to proceed. My usual toolbox was of very little use. Our group was in crises, and I was embarrassed and to be honest ... terrified.

Nine months earlier, I had taken on a new role as a member of a small leadership team that was responsible for an enterprise-wide deployment of a lean management system. This would require a dramatically different way of operating for all leaders in the company. Having spent the previous 15 years in progressively responsible leader roles I was well-versed, if not fairly expert, in the largely traditional view of leadership that had made the company successful for over 100 years. I was aware that this would be a different challenge than any I had faced before. My job before was generally to take something that already existed (a process, team, approach, etc.) and make it better. But this was to be transformative. Until then I operated within the confines of my function; this cut across boundaries, functional, and geographic. I was used to clear lines of authority and decision making; this was stakeholder hell.

My passion for my new role came from my firm belief that this was the right thing to do for the company, our employees, and our customers. I was also completely aligned with the core assumptions about people and how operations could improve customer value. For example, the people doing the work are responsible for fixing the work. Leaders need a systems view of the organization, not silos. Maybe most importantly, I believed that people were inherently motivated and capable. When performance did not meet expectations, I look to the process and system the people are working in first.

So this was an exciting, highly visible new challenge that I believed in completely! What could possibly go wrong?

I was less aware of other important considerations like leadership habits I had accumulated over the years, that, though aligned with the organization at the time, were often totally misaligned with the belief system I espoused. When one of my people was struggling with a project, I was proud of my reputation to jump in and get my hands dirty in the work. I thought I could "save" the project … and the person. I generally knew as much or more about the work, and was as skilled at it, as most anyone in my group. I was a superior technician. I had some knowledge and skills in the lean system we were deploying, although I quickly found out how true the expression "a little knowledge can be dangerous" is. I was schooled to be the expert in my area and to provide answers to problems. This had become the value my internal customers saw in me and that I saw in myself.

My big a-ha moment came to me fairly suddenly and resulted in significant, but mixed, emotions, with two catalysts responsible for it. One was a simulation-based program that, while we had designed it for others, had me as the pilot participant. One of the benefits of a well-facilitated simulation is that you encounter a mirror of your behavior as a leader. The picture in that mirror was not as well-groomed as my self-image! I could easily see how I contributed to a message that the change had to occur in "others," not "us." I talked about the need for keeping a mindset of systemic thinking, but did not practice this myself. This was sobering.

On the other hand, I was simultaneously participating in a corporate-wide executive 360 assessment of the same climate I created in the group. One thing I took away from this experience was that people believed in me and what I stood for (even if I was not always the best practitioner). This let me know that I could reach out to other people for help. I knew I could be open and honest about my personal leadership "gaps" I hoped to close. I knew I could "try on" new behaviors and practices. To my delight, this turned out to be true, and then I found myself in a self-reinforcing cycle. I would share ideas about what I wanted to work on with my team, I would try something, we'd learn something. and then we'd move on. PDCA.

With just a few short months to get up and running, we staffed up, created project plans, and engaged our partners in the business. Training programs were scheduled, materials printed, and communications went out. We had a good plan with plenty of spreadsheets making sure we thought of everything. Then we implemented ... And it was chaos. People were being pulled in many directions. It was stressful, we clearly were not meeting the needs of the business, and all of the good changes we were experimenting with were at risk. We needed to get a handle on intake.

Unfortunately, the intake practices I had used before were largely transactional (submit the form, and we'll get back to you) and were designed in part to allow leadership to control the use of resources (significant asks were reviewed by senior manager team monthly). This, however, was a much more unstable environment that required the ability to anticipate unique needs, make decisions quickly, and find flexible resources we could quickly deploy. We didn't have any of these capabilities.

Following my instincts, I decided to bring the whole team in to talk about the issues we were dealing with. Still, I had no idea of how to understand and solve our problem, let alone prioritize next steps. In retrospect, I see that four important things were going for me.

1. *Having sourced the team internally and externally, I had a diverse group that collectively possessed wide and deep skills.*
2. *I was optimistic and communicated this to the group.*

3. *I was forced to be humble and allow members of the group to take leadership roles in problem solving. My toolbox didn't apply. I didn't know how to fix this.*
4. *We had answers in our work. As we had been developing material for the lean deployment we were, in spite of ourselves, beginning to learn how to apply a new mindset and new practices to our work. There may have been other ways to approach all of this, but this is what we had.*

This entire project forced me into a role where my value was not about being able to solve big problems, but to create the environment where people had the context, time, space, processes, and capabilities to solve problems. I had to be comfortable being absolutely transparent about the big problems we were facing and how we were approaching them. It was hard to say publicly that we were not serving the needs of our customers and not delivering the value the organization should expect. From my experience, these situations meant the leader was not doing his job, should be held accountable, and replaced. These were basic things I had to come to terms with to proceed.

Leveraging the knowledge in the group, my direct reports and I fleshed out how we were going to move forward. We knew we needed to challenge our understanding of who our customers really were and what their needs were. We had to measure how we delivered on these needs (or not), identify the biggest gaps, and start prioritizing action steps. We needed to have a systematic and repeatable way to address our gaps. We needed to work together to do all of these things.

I am happy to say that eventually, we were able to make major changes in our structure, including the roles of people needed to play now that we had a clearer (and shared) understanding of our customers and what we actually did for them. Since new decisions around the work and roles and responsibilities were made in the context of problem solving (on a real business problem) and made collectively by the team, these new decisions just made sense to people. And, for the most part, we were having fun and feeling proud of what we were learning together and making possible for the organization.

The experience for me was transformational. If I had to give advice to other leaders, I'd share the following:

1. **Your management system counts.** *As we iterated our management system, my life and the experience of working with my group*

tangibly improved. Personally, my stress level decreased as I had a clear picture of what problems we were facing and what we were doing about them. As a team, we saw that we were having much more fun together then the teams around us. We felt that we had control over our destiny and were being productive. Now seeing people more engaged and solving problems I could never do on my own, I began to see how I was contributing more as a coach. I developed a new understanding of what it meant to "hold someone accountable." They were accountable to the team, not to me; to solving problems, not just completing specified results.

2. **Be authentic—model the open communication** that reinforces it. More often than not, acknowledging your gaps and your mistakes will encourage others to help. If people can depend on you to be up front, they will take risks with you.

3. **Know what your customer needs are**, measure how you are delivering on them, and make that the base of your problem solving. This provided our magnetic north.

4. **Approach everything with a problem-solving lens**. By the end of the year, everything—from space planning, training needs analyses, to our employee engagement survey responses—was guided by a systematic and shared problem-solving process.

5. **Developing capabilities in your group,** and cross-training in particular, are your best friends. Again, it's great to support people in their self-guided development by funding training etc. What's better is to build targeted skills in the right people, which explicitly enables you to address gaps in the delivery of value to your customers.

In the end, my self-image, which I had developed over years of experience and supported by 360 assessments and other feedback, was that I was a leader who listens, never micromanages, and generally cares about the people he works with. I was curious and hard-working with decent relationships across the business. What I learned was that these are, at best, necessary but not sufficient conditions. Being placed in an environment where my approach just wasn't working was a wake-up call for me. I was shocked out of complacency. Thankfully, I had a foundation to build upon. People generally trusted me and were willing to give me the benefit of the doubt. This helped me take risks.

For me, the big opportunity was to change the management system I created for the team to get work done . . . to facilitate more discussion and *make fewer decisions. My responsibility was to lead the collective process of building of a management architecture that would enable the team constantly get better at knowing their customers and creating value. How did this contrast with where I started? I wasn't standing in front of a group of people looking at me for the answer. I was around a table with a team of talented, engaged people solving problems that we had forced ourselves to understand. I was not afraid of problems and how my leadership would react. I had confidence that we would find our way through whatever we were facing as long as we stuck to the principles of the new management system. As time passed and we all naturally moved on from this particular team, I carry these insights into every professional challenge I encounter and they continue to serve me well. Oh what a learning experience it has been.*

Our view: Mike's story speaks to several themes we've covered in this book. He had his own unique awakening which led to the realization that he needed to change. Mike focused on team-based problem solving and learned how to deploy problem responsibility. As a result, he transformed into a humble, engaging leader who created a safe environment for his team to grow and become successful. They soon began having a lot more fun serving their internal customers.

LOCKED IN MY OFFICE

By Karl Ohaus

Sometimes One Simple Experiment Can Get You Right to the Root Cause of a Problem

One moment of particular clarity that I remember was when I was the president of a company that was three years into its Lean transformation. If you had visited the facility you would have seen visual management, standard work, flow of materials, and plenty of information. If you stayed long enough you would have noticed a well-organized workplace, predictable and effective change overs, a system of management, and standard work that quickly identified and elevated problems to be solved. All of these lean tools contributed to a dramatic three-year turnaround of my company.

Sales were up 90%, the operations had gone from 24 hours 7 days a week to 20 hours 5 days a week. Lead times from order of new product to *full production was 30% of the industry average, and we made this process stable. But in spite of these good results, we still had a long list of improvements we wanted to make. As we learned more about our ability to understand the work, there was no question that we saw more and more opportunities to improve. We began to see new problems that had always been there, but we just did not see them before. Everything sounded and looked great, but outside of our view, there was still a problem. I was exhausted, and it seemed like **every problem eventually required me getting involved.***

My teacher (sensei) was a no nonsense, ex-Navy seal named Ben. Over three years we had built a great relationship. As I learned, he learned, and then he challenged me to learn even more! I called Ben to seek his wisdom.

*It had been many months since we talked, and he appeared excited to make a visit to our facility. After a brief walk through operations, Ben suggested we go back to my office and discuss what we saw. It was clear that Ben saw something that had been a blind spot for me. I asked, **"What do you think the problem is?"** And without hesitation, Ben said, **"YOU."** You are too willing to take problem responsibility away from your people. You walk the shop floor looking for problems to solve and you're very good at it. Why would anyone that works in your shop solve their own problems when they can have you do it for them?*

*The short-term solution was simple. **Ben locked me in my office the next morning** and posted the following notice across the plant.*

> *Karl will be in his office all day. If you have a problem, please try to solve it yourself. If you have exhausted all possible resources and the problem needs to be discussed with Karl, please come to Karl to explain.*

*All day long, no one came to my door, and we had a record production day. This was my big a-ha moment. It was a simple, but hard lesson to learn: Help when help is actually needed, and more than anything, **leave responsibility with the actual problem solvers!***

Our view: This story speaks to personal awakening and creating respectful connections that we discussed in Chapters 2 and 7. Karl struggled with letting go of his highly developed skill of problem solving, but through an abrupt awakening he learned how to finally deploy problem responsibility to his organization.

PROBLEM SOLVING FOR COMPLEXITY WITH AN ENERGIZED CROSS-FUNCTIONAL TEAM

by Kimberly Hannon

In 2011, I was hired as Manager of Lease Administration Data & Billing at American Tower. Founded in 1995, American Tower, is one of the largest global Real Estate Investment Trusts (REITs), is a leading independent owner, operator, and developer of wireless and broadcast communications real estate. My teams ensure that the billing for services and fees associated with getting carriers onto one of our sites, as well as the recurring rent to collocate on the site, is done in a timely and accurate way. Since inception of the Lease Administration Organization, the size of American Tower, and thus the size of my team, as well as the scope of what they are responsible for, has changed considerably.

Our global portfolio includes nearly over 170,000 communications sites, including nearly 41,000 properties in the United States and more than 129,000 properties internationally. Headquartered in Boston, Massachusetts, we have offices across the United States and in 16 countries across the globe. As is typical with any company undergoing such rapid growth, we found ourselves with a number of inherited/de-centralized processes and legacy systems. This led to manual work, rework, and risk to data quality. Over the years, we have made numerous process improvements, however, we still faced many complexities and system limitations that resulted in less than optimal results; namely within the work stream that involved billing our customers for services and fees associated with getting them onto one of our sites.

We were embarking upon an IT project that would provide us with a system enhancement, however, before moving forward, we decided to take a deeper, objective look at the end to end processes that would touch this system; and ensure we weren't simply automating a less than optimal process. In July 2018, we brought in Jim Luckman of Lean Transformations Group to facilitate a Value Stream Improvement (VSI) initiative for us. The goal of this project was to examine the end to end processes across multiple functional areas including: Site Development, Leasing Operations, and Services & Fees Billing teams.

During our workshop, we identified the key suppliers and customers of this work stream, as well as outputs. We estimated the total time involved, as well as the percentage of complete and accurate outputs. We looked at rework. What was striking was seeing this process drawn up on the white board and defects so clearly called out. This helped us zero in on where we could concentrate on, in order to make the most impact. It helped to have all of the teams involved in this work stream in the same room, hearing the same message. It didn't take long before we all started to gain a better understanding of how we were all connected.

From this initial workshop, we designated goals to individual goal owners. These corresponded to the defects that we had called out in the work stream. Focusing on improving our complete and accuracy percentages, we decided that there were areas where we simply couldn't track meaningful metrics, for example, in our purchase order logging function. So, this was step one: create a process and interim system that would provide us data to measure and use to make decisions based upon what the story of the data told us.

As our VSI project progressed, what struck me was the ability of our team to change direction and self-organize, based upon the learnings we had in the four weeks leading up to the next read out session. For example, we found that entering every single data point into our interim system wouldn't give us the value that would warrant the time spent on data entry. Using PDCA, we learned to adapt and implement changes as necessary.

Upon completion of our 90-day read-out, I felt like we not only took steps to address the immediate needs, but we worked together to create a road map to get us to our long-term ideal state. This also provided my team members with the tools necessary to lead process initiatives in their respective areas. We strengthened partnerships between all groups involved, which I know will help us all function much more effectively. For me, this project provided me with leadership opportunities that I have not had before.

Our view: The Value-Stream approach provides the foundation for collaborative problem-solving. In this case, Kimberly led a cross-functional team that demonstrated their ability to self-organize and take advantage of the characteristics of complex adaptive systems.

HUMBLE LEADERSHIP WITH NOT-SO-HUMBLE RESULTS

A Story of Sister Paula Marie Buley Captured by Olga Flory

Rivier is a non-profit catholic university in Nashua, New Hampshire. It was founded in 1933 as an all-women's college for the daughters of mill workers and became a co-educational institution in 1991. For decades, it attracted, on most part, students from the New England region, offering an opportunity to earn undergraduate degrees in liberal arts, education, business, and nursing. Its academic programs had a good reputation and fees were reasonable. The campus was nice, yet somewhat understated. Rivier values were strong and unaffected by time and/or external events. Rooted in its traditions, the College settled in its routine and didn't seem to have changed much over the years. And then something happened. In 2011, a new President came to take the lead at Rivier. Her name was Sister Paula Marie Buley.

Catholicism is hardly associated with change—it is rooted in stability and tradition, yet under Sister Paula's leadership, Rivier began to transform. The first significant change came in 2012 with an upgrade from a college to a university status. Rivier's programs began to grow through the addition of a number of doctoral, graduate, and undergraduate degrees. Online education became an integral part of the university curricula. Rivier began to expand its global outreach to create opportunities for students to study abroad and to bring young people from other countries to study at Rivier.

The next wave of transformations included renovations to campus grounds. According to Sister Paula, Rivier programs were superb but the campus did not reflect the quality of education. By transforming the campus, she was trying to establish a subliminal comparison to how a person gets transformed through education at Rivier. Renovation of the alumni legacy garden, admissions welcome center, and campus quad; creation of the Heritage Plaza; improved lighting and signage; manicured lawns and brick walkways ... In just a few years, the look of the campus changed drastically. It became welcoming and dignified, and, more importantly, it began to communicate pride for education-inspired transformation of hearts and minds of Rivier students.

Most recently, the University broke ground on the construction of a new athletics pavilion and renovation of the university softball field, and created plans to replace an outdated 60-year-old science facility with a new 30,000-square-foot Science Center to ensure students have access to the most up-to-date technologies and equipment.

While all these changes were happening in different parts of Rivier's operation, none of them were random. They were based on a deep understanding of what in the business world we call "the voice of the customer." Sister Paula doesn't use the language of leadership books and management consultants. She simply believes that "they (the Board, administration, staff, and faculty) need to see how our students see" in order to understand what they look for in a higher educational institution and make sure that the university meets their needs. When she came to Rivier, Sister Paula engaged her team in the analysis of the needs of Rivier students and the review of student application and enrollment patterns. What they learned was that the most desirable features for students and applicants are technology, collaborative learning, and athletic programs and facilities. Understanding customer needs informed a change plan that Sister Paula and her team developed to initiate Rivier transformation.

*What kind of a leader does it take to transform a small provincial college into a blooming growing university? Sister Paula's view on leadership is simple. She believes that **leadership is a combination of motivation and experience.***

*Her personal motivation has always been "to do good and to be good, **to work with others toward a common goal,**" and, relative to the work in higher education, "help bring an institution to a higher and better state" (Rivier's motto is "Altiora et Meliora." Translated from Latin, it means "higher and better"). And she certainly has an ability to engage everybody in generating common goals and creating a vision for the higher and better state. In meetings, Sister Paula prefers to listen more than speak herself, making sure that everybody's voice is heard and encouraging what she calls "messy discussions." "On the one hand, it is my role to control messiness," she says. "On the other hand, one needs to have messy conversations before you get to a solution." "It is just like cooking," she adds. "You need messiness to get to a final proportion of ingredients." This collaborative approach to shaping a future-state vision allowed Sister Paula and her team to come up with four strategic priorities:*

- *Global engagement*
- *Employment promise*
- *Creation of the Center for Behavioral Health Professions and Workforce Development, and*
- *Strength-based wellbeing*

The number of priorities could easily be more than four considering how many ideas everybody brought to the table. But Sister Paula believes that it is "more important to think it through than to think it up" (focus on the vital few!), which is why she wants to make sure they go deep on the initiatives and get them accomplished before they set up the next set of priorities.

"It's a privilege to work with Sister Paula," says Karen Cooper, Vice President for University Advancement. "Everyone is part of the team and we move forward together with the same vision for our future."

*With strategic direction in place, Sister Paula now wants to make sure that the execution of every initiative is a result of **collaborative thinking and doing.** "You can't lead people to where they don't want to go," she says. It is not enough for a leader to create an attractive vision. It is the ability to build consensus around it that matters. She learned this lesson many years ago when, in 1996, she came up with an initiative to distribute laptop computers to students to help them learn better and faster with technology, to give them, as she called it "a window to the world." Considering laptops were a novelty and, hence, quite expensive, she knew it wouldn't be easy to get this proposal approved. So she did some prep work to build support for the project. In her own words, what she learned from it was that*

> *it is not the meeting where you present the idea but the meeting before the meeting that matters. A meeting in which you draw people in to consensus, **draw people in to having a share of the future state** and having a share of creating something new.*

Sister Paula doesn't know the term Nemawashi but she executes it beautifully, demonstrating respect for people by engaging them in solving problems and making critical decisions.

> *In Japanese, Nemawashi (根回し) means an informal process of quietly laying the foundation for some proposed change or project, by talking to the people concerned, gathering support and feedback, and so forth. Successful nemawashi enables changes to be carried out with the consent of all sides. Source: Wikipedia*

Regarding the experience component of leadership, it is not comprised of the jobs that Sister Paula has had in her life, although she has had a few. Prior to establishing herself as a senior leader in higher education, she worked as a waitress, a guitar teacher, and a claims rep in an insurance company. However, it is not what she has done but what she has *"learned from doing things well and from not doing things well"* that shaped her as a leader. One important lesson was about leadership influence: when a leader needs to be in control and exert influence, and when he/she needs to let it go. Of course, there is a story behind it!

At the time when Sister Paula served as VP of Finance at Immaculata University, she got to run a project for building a new library. It was supposed to be a beautiful building and she felt excited and proud to have an opportunity to lead this work. One day, she was taking a group of Board members on a tour of the library. The building was still under construction, the workers were pouring concrete, as the group—all in hard hats and safety boots—was taking a walk around it. Because Sister Paula was so deeply involved in the project and loved the future library, she wanted them to understand how beautiful it was going to be, so she kept providing—with a great deal of enthusiasm!—more and more details about the project. Until one of the Sisters who also accompanied the group turned to her and told her to turn it down a notch. "Cool it," she said. "Your enthusiasm is overwhelming the experience of us being in the library."

This incident may seem minor but it had a profound effect on Sister Paula. She realized that she was pushing them to get excited instead of creating an opportunity for their enthusiasm to develop organically. By leading the walk and sharing information that she though they needed to know she was trying to control the outcomes of the walk thus taking away an opportunity for the group to experience the beauty of the building and understanding the importance of the project on their own terms.

Her leadership has had a remarkable impact on how people at Rivier connect and communicate, build, and maintain relationships, and how they engage in a continuous effort to improve everything they do. Rivier had always had a warm family-like atmosphere. Talking to staff, faculty, students, one couldn't help but get a vibe of a great community of like-minded individuals. What Sister Paula has contributed to it is a belief that this community can achieve anything. That she is there to support them and work with them but that it is essentially up to them to take the university to the future. She calls Rivier an institution without a ceiling and works hard to turn this belief into the foundation of a new organizational culture.

Our view: As described in Chapter 7, if leaders can be respectful with their people and provide alignment, great things will happen. That is exactly what happened with Sister Paula. This story is about a remarkable leader who achieved extraordinary results with a simple but focused leadership principle: trust the people, align the people, support the people, let the diverse creativity emerge, and remove the limits of their thinking.

BUILDING EXCITEMENT THROUGH ENGAGING PEOPLE IN PROBLEM SOLVING

By Adrian Verduzco, Operations Director, Raytheon

In early 2018, Raytheon Missile Systems (RMS) launched a key initiative to revive and improve its Lean operating system. Over the last decade, we've established a Lean management system at Raytheon that is focused on a tiered accountability meetings and visual controls. To design this system we established a centralized Lean deployment team to develop standards, training, and tools. In addition, our leadership team and middle managers participated in Lean benchmarking events.

Early on, these benchmarking engagements offered insight to "best in class" Lean companies. In many cases, RMS was able to emulate best practices from these companies to yield immediate improvement in our value streams. Additionally, the Lean deployment team offered dedicated resources to teach, implement, and provide short-term sustainment of Lean concepts, tools, learning, and best practices. However, over time, natural business entropy led to less than optimal sustainment of the system. The tiered accountability structure became a means of status rather than a method to solve problems and drive action. I noticed that the Lean deployment team was impacted by natural attrition of talent, which is why it was ultimately disbanded. In order to quickly rectify the situation, my team and I launched a new initiative.

To reinvigorate our Lean management system, we chartered a new team of high performers from across the organization to think through our strategic priorities once more. This team quickly adopted a change management playbook and began to develop targeted improvements to solve the perceived deficiencies associated with the accountability process and visual controls. We aimed to create a set of standards that everyone would be able to follow in order reset our behaviors where we knew we were deficient. But as we began to engage the rest of our organization in *this new work, we realized that our challenge was different than we thought. The true root cause of our issue was that we had lost focus on Lean fundamentals and, more importantly, the **concept of engaging all employees to solve problems**. Through our partnership with the Lean Transformations Group we redirected our initiative to address our issue both from the "top down" and from the "bottom up."*

*The way we would support the new "bottom-up" approach would be to engage directly with our multi-disciplined value stream teams with the goal of coaching folks to use value stream thinking to identify impactful problems at the delivery point and then solve them. Through these focused learning sessions we began to **organically grow problem solvers**. We saw assembly technicians, support staff, and front-line leaders become newly engaged. We emphasized that experimentation was acceptable and "quick wins" were better than getting it perfect down the road. As we matured, our focus became about learning how to sustain regular reflection sessions that could support us in the Deming cycle of plan–do–check–adjust.*

*Our "top-down" approach focused on our leadership team and middle managers. Our new goal was to expose these leaders to our new "bottom-up" philosophy, define their roles as **problem-solving coaches**, and teach techniques for effective coaching. We set aside teams to help these leaders practice problem solving and coaching using humble inquiry. In addition, we took a subset of our leadership team and middle managers on a benchmarking trip to a company where we felt the leadership team embodied new desired coaching behaviors. This trip energized the team and sparked immediate behavioral changes in leadership style, management routines, and Lean thinking.*

Over the course of several months, we were able to engage several factory areas with these new simultaneous "top-down" and "bottom-up" approaches. In these areas our value stream teams increased output, stabilized the frequency of deliveries, reduced overtime, and created a more inclusive environment for problem solving. We saw employees become more excited about their work and leaders build on this excitement to set new goals and solve problems. This shift away from "implementing Lean" to encouraging bottom-up problem solving coupled with a better understanding of Lean fundamentals has proven to be effective for us at Raytheon.

Lastly, and most importantly, our leadership team is now keenly aware of their role in our Lean learning and organizational transformation.

Although new learning is uncomfortable, we have started to change the way we think about our role as leaders. We see the difference between classic command-and-control leadership versus coaching through humble inquiry. We've changed the way we look at results-based metrics. We understand that we can coach our teams to focus on continuous and disciplined problem-solving rather than reacting to results orientated metrics. The problem-solving process will create results. For me, I have been able to apply my new learning to so much more than my work on Lean learning. All of these new skills have helped me improve as a mentor and tackle complex business challenges. Like everything in life, discipline is required to develop new habits. I know it's through continued practice that I will see more results.

Our view: This story is about a team that had a paradigm shift from blanket solutions to developing problem-solving teams. Adrian led a small team of leaders who had the task to reengage the operations group in the Lean principles, something that lost energy over the years. This group, first, got themselves to embrace a problem-solving mindset. Then, they used that thinking to narrow their focus on the few higher leverage areas to change the culture: 1) engagement at the line level, and 2) leadership understanding of their new role. Most impressively, this team modeled leadership for the paradigm of Problem Solving for Complexity. From their actions, the rest of the organization is evolving into the same paradigm. This is a great example of growing a new culture by modeling the behaviors.

Conclusion

"Never doubt that a small group of thoughtful, committed citizens can change the world. Indeed, that is all who ever have."

Margaret Mead

A MODERN-DAY ENLIGHTENMENT?

After writing this book, we had to ask ourselves: Is this paradigm shift we're talking about a new problem or is it the same kind of problem Western society experienced during the period of enlightenment where the change was about people using reason rather than blindly following the rules of one all-knowing individual?

In the late 1700s, Immanuel Kant provided the following definition of enlightenment:

> "Enlightenment is release from his self-incurred tutelage. Tutelage is man's inability to make use of his understanding without directions from another. Self-incurred is the tutelage when its cause lies not in lack of reason but in lack of resolution and courage to use it without direction from another. Sapere aude!" Have the courage to use your own reason!— That is the motto of enlightenment.

Kant was addressing the problem of the centuries-old practice of serfdom where the peasants were indebted to their lords. Peasants had no voice and were blindly serving their master's will. Surfs could be bought and sold, often were abused, could not leave their lord's land, and they had no rights. Kant believed that the peasants were part of the problem by passively accepting their condition. But he also believed that nothing would change if the lords did not acknowledge the need for freedom and enable a new enlightened paradigm to emerge.

Whether or not we have language for it, we understand that emergence happens. It's a wonderful thing that it does, otherwise we'd still be living with serfdom.

What about today's typical organization though? Are we *truly* free to challenge the directions from above? Are we engaged in a shared experience with others to collectively grasp problem situations? Are we given the space to learn our way through business challenges, create solutions to problems as we go? In the Blanket Solutions paradigm, the voice of the individual is hugely limited, because people are not encouraged to contribute to a shared vision of problem situations. Individuals lack the courage to step outside the confines of the system restrictions that limit the individuals' ability to learn, grow, and challenge the status quo. Come to think of it, the problems organizations experience today look a lot like the problems people experienced during the enlightenment period.

We might say, the current complex adaptive system of our world—and our growing awareness of how to navigate and work within complex adaptive systems—elevates us to a *new* kind of enlightenment, one that drives us to spend more time interacting in our social network to uncover interdependent root causes of system problems. This interaction is important because we believe that work, for everybody, should just be more interesting, rewarding, and fun. Since we live in a more complex and uncertain world, we have many opportunities every day to uncover new clues and create learning experiments, engaging others in the search for objective truth in any given problem situation. This continuous discovery process can serve as a way to honor individual voices and make everyone more enthusiastic about their work and their lives. Here is your opportunity to cross the barrier into the new paradigm, venture into the unknown, and lead the modern-day enlightenment.

You can take advantage of your understanding of complex adaptive systems and like the termite, hey, roll that first dirt ball! You can begin learning through the lens of problem solving for complexity. You can use the concepts from this book to begin creating something new and exciting. And then you and your team can decide where you want to take all this new learning.

CAPTURING THE LESSONS FROM THIS BOOK

Leaders lead the paradigm shift. Paradigms exist, and we live inside them without even thinking about them. We automatically act out of habits that are consistent with the paradigm.

In this book, we have covered concepts and actions that are intended to help you transition your organization from your existing paradigm to a new paradigm. We believe the new paradigm is in better alignment with the new world order, fast paced, changing, and full of uncertainty. You learned three concepts intended to change your thinking and prepare you for leading in today's world.

First, complex adaptive systems, is a model that is better aligned with the fast-paced, unpredictable context we all live in and work in. Your organization, also a complex adaptive system, needs to be managed to take advantage of *nonlinearity* and *emergence* that are characteristic of these systems.

Second, two different paradigms provide the contrast between today and what you should expect from an intentional transition.

Third, the assumptions of each paradigm give you a way to examine and think deeply about what needs to change.

You learned a three high-leverage leadership actions you can use to evolve the assumptions of your organization from those of the Imposing Blanket Solutions paradigm to those of the Problem Solving for Complexity paradigm. We shared with you the approach for building a framework for solving problems with a focus on the process for delivering value to the customer instead of the wasteful habits of reacting to short-term results, especially making more profit. You were given a communications practice of humble inquiry that not only shows respect to the people in your organization, but also cherishes their diversity in thinking, making them cohesive, problem-solving teams.

Finally, we gave you, the king or queen of learning, some suggestions on how to create an organization of learners who use a systems approach to solve business problems. As the leader of the paradigm shift, we hope you learned that the personal challenge of changing your own habits, practiced in small experiments together, with your people, is what creates real culture change.

THE LEARNING DOESN'T STOP HERE

As you grow and learn, of course, you will encounter problems we have not directly addressed in this book. Over the years, we have seen these problems emerge as the Problem Solving for Complexity paradigm begins to make an impact. But through the continued practice, when these issues arise, you will be able to easily manage them.

Here are some problems you are likely to encounter as you shift paradigms:

- **The problem of living in two paradigms simultaneously.** From the start, you will find out you need to act and behave in concert with the new paradigm and the old paradigm at the same time. When you are interacting with others that are not a part of your transition effort, it is advantageous to stay in their existing paradigm. They will not understand your new behaviors and ultimately will dismiss you. You cannot be a zealot and try to influence the others. It will not work. You need to find the right time and method for engaging others.
- **The problem of root causes being a part of your policies and procedures.** Some of the root causes you find in your new problem-solving processes will be deeply embedded in your current policies and procedures. They simply manifest themselves as disruptions of flow in your value streams. An example of a widely held policy is the performance review based on individual performance. This policy is a reductionist concept that is attempting to improve the performance of individuals, a concept that is not embraced by systems thinking. Individual performance improvements often cause uneven flow in value streams. There are many policies that need to be questioned and changed to support the more holistic Problem Solving for Complexity paradigm.
- **The problem of blanket solutions being imposed on you and your team** while you are building a problem solving for complexity culture. The rest of the organization, those parts that have not been actively engaged in experimenting with the new paradigm, will continue to impose their blanket solutions thinking on you. Just expect it and be prepared for it. These overlapping initiatives

may cause conflicts and confusion that you will need to address. But you can do it! It's all part of the learning.

- **The problem of other departments impacting your value streams.** How to effectively engage support functions will eventually become an issue. At some point, you will discover that the biggest problem gaps you have may be caused by support teams. You can use your problem-solving process and your effective communications skills to draw these groups into your problem situation, helping them to see how they contribute to your customer delivery problem. This will help their business, too.

- **The problem of resistance to learning.** How to effectively create high-leverage learning across the organization can be addressed through the so-called Integration Events. When you bring together diverse groups to share their experiences, you accelerate the organic growth of organizational learning. This is the same concept of connecting nodes across the Internet. Where there is high traffic, there are shared concepts and growth. We recommend bringing people together in a common physical space first before you move to blogs. Being in the same proximity will provide an opportunity for practicing respectful communications. It can also create an enormous amount of necessary goodwill.

WHAT YOU CAN EXPECT AS YOU AIM TO CREATE THE CONDITIONS FOR MEANINGFUL CHANGE AND BETTER PERFORMANCE

Culture change is considered a long-term process, but we have seen evidence that this statement is misleading. By approaching culture change using the characteristics of complex adaptive systems where the butterfly effect is accepted (a small perturbance in initial conditions makes a large change later), focused groups working on solving real problems with the support and guidance of the leader, can actually make change very quickly. We have observed this rapid change effect with small cross-functional teams (up to 30 people), functions (over 100 people), and sites like separate plants (over 1,000 people). The pace of change depends on many things, and in part, it depends on you.

You, the leader, should be the aforementioned small perturbance. You have the opportunity to model effective problem-solving thinking and a deeply respectful style of communications. Culture change takes place from the bottom-up so change is about how you show up with the "lower-level" people in your organization. The leverage point in complex adaptive systems is at the local interaction level where you are with your people. Emergence happens because of many local interactions and improved social connections.

You are the key to creating new local interactions and you set the standard for respect and trust. In other words, once again, your biggest challenge is you. Making that decision to transform yourself is the first big step. Then, once you do that, everything changes. A new breathtaking world opens up to you for you to delight in satisfying your thirst for knowledge. Caterpillars cannot imagine what life is like to be a butterfly. Once you have been awakened and become a butterfly, pleasure comes from watching others make the same transformation and join you on your never-ending journey of making a better life for you and all those around you. You can lead the way to a modern-day enlightenment!

Deep Dive

The purpose of this chapter is to offer a deeper look into your own personal problem situation. Each chapter has 1) Questions for Reflection and 2) Further Study which offers a few of the best resources for enhancing your understanding.

INTRODUCTION

Questions for Reflection

After you just scanned through the Introduction, it may be too much to ask of you to determine which of the paradigms influences you and your organization. However, we would like you to start thinking about it.

YOUR CURRENT CULTURE:

- How can you define the culture?
- What supports and what hinders problem solving in your organization?
- Who makes decisions about what is a problem and how it needs to be solved?
- Who solves problems?
- What is your most critical problem in delivering either a product or service to your external customer? Which functions contribute to the problem?

YOU:

- What is your motivation for solving problems?
- Think about the latest problem you solved. What was your approach to understanding it? How did you select the solution? What happened when the solution was implemented?

- What was the last leadership book you have read? What have you learned? What have you been able to apply? How has it worked?
- Many companies have attempted to become Lean. If your organization has been deploying Lean tools, what is working, what is not working?

Further Study

- "Age of Transition, Paradigm Shift," Amazon Video
- "The Structure of Scientific Revolutions," Thomas Kuhn
- "Complex Adaptive Systems," Dr. Chantell Beatey, Kindle
- "Complex Adaptive Organizations": https://youtu.be/EFv-
- "Complex Adaptive Systems": www.businessdictionary.com/definition/complex-adaptive-system-CAS.html
- "What's Lean Principles": www.lean.org/WhatsLean/Principles.cfm
- "Edgar Schein Model of Organizational Culture": www.managementstudyguide.com/edgar-schein-model.htm

CHAPTER 1—THE NEW ROLE OF THE LEADER

Questions for Reflection

YOUR ORGANIZATION

- How can you describe the management philosophy?
- What have you observed about change in your organization? Who led it? How was it managed?
- How does your organization ensure employee engagement?

YOU

- What are your highly developed skills? What are your lesser developed skills? How do your skills relate to being the change master in your organization?
- Whose approach to leadership is more aligned with your beliefs and values: Walt Disney's or Jack Welch's?

- How can you describe your leadership style? Who or what has helped you shape this style?
- What might it feel like to venture into a completely unknown world?

Further Study

- "Employee Engagement Research (Master List of 32 Findings)." Kevin Kruse, https://www.kevinkruse.com/employee-engagement-research-master-list-of-29-studies/.
- "These 4 Principles Drive Disney's Organizational Culture." Equities.com. www.equities.com/news/these-4-principles-drive-disney-s-organizational-culture.
- "The Hero's Journey—Mythic Structure of Joseph Campbell's Monomyth": www.movieoutline.com/articles/the-hero-journey-mythic-structure-of-joseph-campbell-monomyth.html

CHAPTER 2—FROM CATERPILLAR TO BUTTERFLY

This chapter is about a personal transformation, so this is an opportunity for you to do some deep soul searching and, maybe, understand something new about yourself.

Questions for Reflection

YOU:

- Have you ever experienced a Eureka moment? What was it associated with? How did it feel? What happened after it?
- Have you ever experienced a painful awakening moment? What caused it? What did it result in?
- Once you realized the need to change something about you, what did the transformation process look like? What did you do? Who helped you? How long did it take until you began to feel comfortable using your new skill/habit?

Further Study

- "Brain Science Behind the A-ha Moment": www.oh-i-see.com/blog/2013/10/10/brain-science-behind-the-aha-moment/
- "The Hero's Journey—Mythic Structure of Joseph Campbell's Monomyth": www.movieoutline.com/articles/the-hero-journey-mythic-structure-of-joseph-campbell-monomyth.html

---

CHAPTER 3—COMPLEX ADAPTIVE SYSTEMS

Questions for Reflection

YOUR ORGANIZATION:

- Can you recall a situation where you could establish a simple cause-and-effect connection? What situation was it?
- What are some examples of interdependent factors that cause a change? How do they affect each other?
- Think about an effective team that you have in your organization. How do the people interact with each other? How do they adjust to different conditions or changes? How is the leadership determined? Is the team operating under command and control or distributed and evolving leadership?
- What characteristics of a complicated system have you observed or experienced in your organization?
- What characteristics of a complex adaptive system have you noticed? What happened when you realized you were inside a complex adaptive system?

YOU:

- How do you feel about the concept of a "leaderless team"? What experiment can you run that will allow you to test this concept?
- What do you think will happen if you "stop leading"?
- What example of emergence (the sum being greater than the parts) can you recall from your leadership practice? What impact did it have on you?

Further Study

- "Simple vs. Complicated vs. Complex vs. Chaotic." NOOP.NL. http://noop.nl/2008/08/simple-vs-complicated-vs-complex-vs-chaotic.html.
- Stacey, Ralph D., and Chris Mowles. *Strategic Management and Organisational Dynamics: The Challenge of Complexity to Ways of Thinking about Organisations*. Harlow, England: Pearson Education, 2016.

CHAPTER 4—TWO PARADIGMS

Questions for Reflection

YOUR ORGANIZATION:

- What are the drivers behind your efforts? Are there *goals*? How are they *measured*? Are they driven from the top of the organization? Are they connected to each other? How do they relate to a business problem?
- Think about some recently implemented initiatives. What problem(s) have they helped solve?
- What business problem would you select to start moving your organization away from blanket solutions?

YOU:

- What blanket solutions have you implemented in your leadership practice? What were the drivers behind the decisions to select those solutions?
- What effects of blanket solutions have you experienced? What was your response to them?
- Which paradigm, do you think, has had more influence on you throughout your life? What led you to this conclusion?

Further Study

- "How Do You Change a Paradigm?" Moonsong. www.moonsong.com.au/how-do-you-change-a-paradigm/.

- "How to Change a Paradigm." Proctor Gallagher Institute. www. proctorgallagherinstitute.com/6104/how-to-change-a-paradigm.

CHAPTER 5—ASSUMPTIONS

There are no questions for reflection for this chapter because we included them at the end of each section inside the chapter.

Results Vs. Means

Further Study

- Denning, Steve. "The Origin of 'The World's Dumbest Idea': Milton Friedman." Forbes. July 05, 2013. Accessed August 8, 2018. www. forbes.com/sites/stevedenning/2013/06/26/the-origin-of-the-worlds-dumbest-idea-milton-friedman/.
- "Toyota Global Site | Customer First Spirit Delivers Quality." Accessed February 2, 2016. www.toyota-global.com/company/ toyota_traditions/philosophy/mar_sep_2010.html

Fragmented Vs. Systems

Further Study

- Cabrera, Derek, and Laura Cabrera. *Systems Thinking Made Simple: New Hope for Solving Wicked Problems.* New York: Plectica Publishing, 2018.
- "From Mechanistic to Social Systemic Thinking." The Systems Thinker. November 19, 2015. Accessed January 25, 2019. https:// thesystemsthinker.com/from-mechanistic-to-social-systemic-thinking/.

- Meadows, Donella H., and Diana Wright. *Thinking in Systems: A Primer.* White River Junction, VT: Chelsea Green Publishing, 201

Control Vs. Responsiveness

Further Study

- Hounshell, David A. "The Same Old Principles in the New Manufacturing." Harvard Business Review. https://hbr.org/1988/11/the-same-old-principles-in-the-new-manufacturing.
- Stacey, Ralph D., and Chris Mowles. *Strategic Management and Organizational Dynamics the Challenge of Complexity to Ways of Thinking about Organizations.* Harlow, United Kingdom: Pearson Education, 2016.

Blame Vs. Inquiry

Further Study

- Gupta, Ashim. "Defensive Reasoning." Practical Management. http://practical-management.com/Organization-Development/Defensive-Reasoning.html.
- "Overcoming Defensive Routines in the Workplace." The Systems Thinker: https://thesystemsthinker.com/overcoming-defensive-routines-in-the-workplace/

Knower Vs. Learner

Further Study

- "Confessions of a Recovering Knower." The Systems Thinker. February 08, 2018: https://thesystemsthinker.com/confessions-of-a-recovering-knower/.
- "The Contribution of Teams to Organizational Learning ..." www.researchgate.net/publication/296638359_The_Contribution_of_Teams_to_Organizational_Learning

CHAPTER 6—BUILD THE FRAMEWORK FOR PROBLEM SOLVING

Questions for Reflection

The primary purpose of questions to this chapter is to help you reflect on the state of problem solving in your organization.

- What is your current process for establishing the person responsible for delivery to the customer? How are the functions supporting that individual made aware of their contribution to help that delivery?
- What does your organization consider the standard problem-solving process? Are all functions using the same process?
- Are the primary goals clear in terms of the delivery of value to external customers?
- What is an example of a good problem definition? How is it measured? Where does that problem exist in your organization? Who owns it?

Further Study

- "Mapping to See: Value-Stream Improvement Workshop." Lean. org. Accessed January 26, 2019. www.lean.org/Bookstore/Product Details.cfm?SelectedProductId=162.
- "Perfecting Patient Journeys." Lean.org. Accessed January 26, 2019. www.lean.org/ppj.

CHAPTER 7—GROW RESPECTFUL SOCIAL CONNECTIONS

Questions for Reflection

YOU:

- In a typical meeting with your team, what percentage of communication is dictate, debate, or dialogue?

- What percent of your time in communicating with subordinates are you doing the thinking vs. them doing the thinking?
- How much do you know about your subordinate's life outside work?

Further Study

- Edmonson, Amy C. *Teaming: How Organizations Learn, Innovate, and Compete in the Knowledge Economy.* San Francisco (US): Jossey Bass, 2012.
- Glaser, Judith E. *Conversational Intelligence: How Great Leaders Build Trust and Get Extraordinary Results.* New York, NY: Bibliomotion, 2016.
- Glaser, Judith E. Glaser, Richard D. "The Neurochemistry of Positive Conversations." Harvard Business Review. December 06, 2017. Accessed January 13, 2019. https://hbr.org/2014/06/the-neurochemistry-of-positive-conversations.
- Schein, Edgar H. *Process Consultation Revisited: Building the Helping Relationship.* Reading, MA: Addison Wesley, 2008.
- Schein, Edgar H. *Humble Inquiry: The Gentle Art of Asking Instead of Telling.* San Francisco: Berrett-Koehler Publishers, 2014.

CHAPTER 8—ACCELERATE LEARNING

Questions for Reflection

YOUR ORGANIZATION:

- What type of company are you? PDCA, pDca, Pdca, or pdCA? How much time do you spend in group reflections?
- What is your current process for capturing learning from problem solving?
- What is your current process for sharing learning across the organization?

YOU:

- How often do you reflect on your actions/behaviors?
- What process do you use to reflect?

Further Study

- Answers Ltd. "Experiential Learning: The Act of Learning from Experiences." UKEssays. November 22, 2018. www.ukessays.com/essays/education/experiential-learning-the-act-of-learning-from-experiences-education-essay.php.
- Edmondson, Amy C. "Strategies for Learning from Failure." Harvard Business Review. August 01, 2014https://hbr.org/2011/04/strategies-for-learning-from-failure.
- Garvin, David A. "Building a Learning Organization." Harvard Business Review. August 01, 2014. https://hbr.org/1993/07/building-a-learning-organization.
- "Kolb Experiential Learning Cycle." Cognitive Learning Strategies | Wentworth Institute of Technology. January 03, 2019. https://wit.edu/lit/engage/kolb-cycle.

CHAPTER 9—START WITH YOURSELF

Reflection

The purpose of this chapter is to help you identify your lesser developed skills and structure your practice. Which is why all reflection questions focus on

YOU:

- What are your lesser developed skills relative to your ability to lead change?
- What small experiments are you running this week to build your skills?
- Who is helping you with your practice?

Further Study

- Coyle, Daniel. *The Talent Code: Greatness Isn't Born. It's Grown. Here's How.* New York: Bantam Books, 2009.
- Kahneman, Daniel. *Thinking, Fast and Slow.* New York: Farrar, Straus and Giroux, 2015.

Bibliography

Ackoff, Russell Lincoln. *Ackoffs Best: Irreverent Reflections on Business and Management*. New York: Wiley, 1999.

"Ackoff's Best: His Classic Writings on Management". Amazon. Accessed January 25, 2019. www.amazon.com/Ackoffs-Best-Classic-Writings-Management/dp/0471316342.

"Alasdair MacIntyre - 9/10. Philosophy for Life. Accessed January 26, 2019. www.philosophyforlife.org/category/alasdair-macintyre/page/9/.

Allen, Will. "Complicated or Complex - Knowing the Difference Is Important. Learning for Sustainability. October 20, 2017. Accessed December 28, 2018. http://learningforsustainability.net/post/complicated-complex/.

Andersen, Erika. "Learning to Learn. Harvard Business Review. September 05, 2018. Accessed December 27, 2018. https://hbr.org/2016/03/learning-to-learn.

Anderson, Dean, and Linda S. Ackerman-Anderson. *Beyond Change Management: How to Achieve Breakthrough Results through Conscious Change Leadership*, Second Edition. San Francisco: Pfeiffer, An Imprent of Wiley, 2010.

Answers Ltd. "Experiential Learning: The Act of Learning from Experiences. UKEssays. November 22, 2018. Accessed December 27, 2018. www.ukessays.com/essays/education/experiential-learning-the-act-of-learning-from-experiences-education-essay.php.

"Aristotle Believed That Happiness Is The End (Telos) Essay Examples". Essay on Should Selling Junk Food in School Canteens Be Banned? – Healt. Accessed January 26, 2019. www.123helpme.com/aristotle-believed-that-happiness-is-the-end-telos–preview.asp?id=511806.

Bacon, Francis, and Joseph Devey. *Novum Organum: Or True Suggestions for the Interpretation of Nature*. New York: Collier, 1902.

Barker, Joel Arthur. *The Business of Paradigms*. Burnsville, MN: Charthouse Learning, 1990.

Berger, Jennifer Garvey. *Changing on the Job: Developing Leaders for a Complex World*. Stanford, CA: Stanford Business Books, 2012.

Bersin, Josh. "5 Keys to Building a Learning Organization. Forbes. January 18, 2012. Accessed December 27, 2018. www.forbes.com/sites/joshbersin/2012/01/18/5-keys-to-building-a-learning-organization/#77cc68a129c4.

Bloomberg.com. Accessed December 27, 2018. www.bloomberg.com/news/articles/2010-02-17/knowing-vs-dot-learning.

Bohm, David Joseph. *On Dialogue: David Bohm*. London: Routledge, 1996.

Byrne, D. S. *Complexity Theory and the Social Sciences: An Introduction*. London: Routledge, 2005.

Cabrera, Derek, and Laura Cabrera. *Systems Thinking Made Simple: New Hope for Solving Wicked Problems*. New York: Plectica Publishing, 2018.

Chichakly, Tabor. "What Are Systems Archetypes? Accessed January 25, 2019. www.iseesystems.com/store/Training/applying-systems-thinking/index.aspx.

Chrismcd, Karl W, and Ennio. "Understanding Complexity". The Great Courses. September 02, 2018. Accessed December 28, 2018. www.thegreatcourses.com/courses/understanding-complexity.html.

Clifford, Catherine. "Jack Welch: This Is the No. 1 Key to Success as a Leader. CNBC. November 17, 2017. Accessed January 24, 2019. www.cnbc.com/2017/11/17/former-ge-ceo-jack-welch-how-to-be-a-great-leader.html.

Cohn, Paulette. "'Walt Before Mickey' Reveals Disney's Persistence Amid Failure. Biography.com. June 16, 2016. Accessed January 24, 2019. www.biography.com/news/walt-before-mickey-walt-disney-movie-2015.

Concepts of Leadership. Accessed December 27, 2018. www.nwlink.com/~donclark/hrd/history/kolb.html.

"Confessions of a Recovering Knower. The Systems Thinker. February 08, 2018. Accessed January 26, 2019. https://thesystemsthinker.com/confessions-of-a-recovering-knower/.

"Confessions of a Recovering Knower. The Systems Thinker. February 08, 2018. Accessed December 27, 2018. https://thesystemsthinker.com/confessions-of-a-recovering-knower/.

"The Contribution of Teams to Organizational Learning. . .. Accessed January 26, 2019. www.researchgate.net/publication/296638359_The_Contribution_of_Teams_to_Organizational_Learning.

Coyle, Daniel. *The Talent Code: Greatness Isnt Born. Its Grown. Heres How*. New York: Bantam Books, 2009.

"Dancing with Systems. The Systems Thinker. March 30, 2016. Accessed January 13, 2019. https://thesystemsthinker.com/dancing-with-systems/.

Dasein, Existentialist. YouTube. May 16, 2014. Accessed January 13, 2019. www.youtube.com/watch?v=2MbigRBKxUU.

Denning, Steve. "The Origin of 'The World's Dumbest Idea': Milton Friedman. Forbes. July 05, 2013. Accessed August 8, 2018. www.forbes.com/sites/stevedenning/2013/06/26/the-origin-of-the-worlds-dumbest-idea-milton-friedman/.

"Did the Jack Welch Model Sow Seeds of G.E.'s Decline ... Accessed January 24, 2019. www.nytimes.com/2017/06/15/business/ge-jack-welch-immelt.html.

"The Difference between Lean and Systems Thinking. Thinkpurpose. February 06, 2015. Accessed January 25, 2019. https://thinkpurpose.com/2015/02/06/the-difference-between-lean-and-systems-thinking/.

Dimoka, Angelika. "What Does the Brain Tell Us About Trust and Distrust? Evidence from a Functional Neuroimaging Study. By Jikun Huang, Ruifa Hu, Scott Rozelle, Fangbin Qiao, Carl E. Pray : SSRN. April 26, 2014. Accessed January 13, 2019. https://papers.ssrn.com/sol3/papers.cfm?abstract_id=2428911.

"Distortion vs Reality. Psychology Today. Accessed January 13, 2019. www.psychologytoday.com/us/articles/200211/distortion-vs-reality.

Dodder, Rebecca, and Robert Dare. *Complex Adaptive Systems and Complexity Theory: Inter-related Knowledge Domains*. Cambridge, MA: MIT, 2000.

Editors. "Germ Theory of Disease - Definition, History and Quiz. Biology Dictionary. May 16, 2017. Accessed January 02, 2019. https://biologydictionary.net/germ-theory/.

Edmondson, Amy C. "Strategies for Learning from Failure. Harvard Business Review. August 01, 2014. Accessed December 27, 2018. https://hbr.org/2011/04/strategies-for-learning-from-failure.

Edmonson, Amy C. *Teaming: How Organizations Learn, Innovate, and Compete in the Knowledge Economy*. San Francisco, CA: Jossey Bass, 2012.

Eidelson, Roy J. "Complex Adaptive Systemsin Behavioral and Social Sciences. Review of General Psychology. May 14, 1996. Accessed June 17, 2014.

"Employee Engagement - The MacLeod Report (by David MacLeod . . .. Accessed January 24, 2019. www.focusgroupevents.com/expert-zone/employee-engagement-the-macleod-report-by-david-macleod-nita-clarke.

"Employee Engagement Research (Master List of 32 Findings). Kevin Kruse. March 06, 2017. Accessed January 24, 2019. www.kevinkruse.com/employee-engagement-research-master-list-of-29-studies/.

"Episode 70: Judith Glaser – Conversational Intelligence. Bregman Partners. Accessed January 13, 2019. http://bregmanpartners.com/podcast/judith-glaser-conversa tional-intelligence/.

Equities.com. "These 4 Principles Drive Disney's Organizational Culture. Equities.com. Accessed January 24, 2019. www.equities.com/news/these-4-principles-drive-disney-s-organizational-culture.

"Eureka! Deconstructing the Brain Mechanics of "Aha!" Moments. Psychology Today. Accessed January 24, 2019. www.psychologytoday.com/us/blog/the-athletes-way/ 201603/eureka-deconstructing-the-brain-mechanics-aha-moments.

"Experiential Learning Cycles Overview of 9 Experiential Learning Cycle Models". Critique of Biological & Evolutionary Processes in Personality. Accessed December 27, 2018. www.wilderdom.com/experiential/elc/ExperientialLearning Cycle.htm.

"From Mechanistic to Social Systemic Thinking. The Systems Thinker. November 19, 2015. Accessed January 25, 2019. https://thesystemsthinker.com/from-mechanistic-to-social-systemic-thinking/.

"From Organizational Learning to the Learning Organization". Journal of Research in Crime and Delinquency. Accessed December 27, 2018. https://journals.sagepub. com/doi/abs/10.1177/1350507698291001.

FutureLearn. "A Review of Common Characteristics of Complex Systems. FutureLearn. Accessed December 28, 2018. www.futurelearn.com/courses/complexity-and-uncer tainty/0/steps/1836.

Garvin, David A. "Building a Learning Organization. Harvard Business Review. August 01, 2014. Accessed December 27, 2018. https://hbr.org/1993/07/building-a-learning-organization.

Gharajedaghi, Jamshid. *Systems Thinking: Managing Chaos and Complexity: A Plat-form for Designing Business Architecture.* Burlington, MA: Morgan Kaufmann, 2011.

Gladwell, Malcolm. *Tipping Point.* Place of Publication Not Identified: Little, Brown, 2014.

Glaser, Judith E. *Conversational Intelligence: How Great Leaders Build Trust and Get Extraordinary Results.* New York: Bibliomotion, 2016.

Glaser, Judith E., and D. Glaser Richard "The Neurochemistry of Positive Conversations. Harvard Business Review. December 06, 2017. Accessed January 13, 2019. https:// hbr.org/2014/06/the-neurochemistry-of-positive-conversations.

Goldstein, Jeffrey, James K. Hazy, and Benyamin B. Lichtenstein. *Complexity and the Nexus of Leadership: Leveraging Nonlinear Science to Create Ecologies of Innovation.* New York: Palgrave Macmillan, 2011.

Gupta, Ashim. "Defensive Reasoning. Practical Management. Accessed January 02, 2019. http://practical-management.com/Organization-Development/Defensive-Reasoning.html.

Hauerwas, Stanley. "The Virtues of Alasdair MacIntyre | Stanley Hauerwas. First Things. October 01, 2007. Accessed March 6, 2016. www.firstthings.com/article/2007/10/ the-virtues-of-alasdair-macintyre.

"Have You Experienced 'Eureka' Moments? Psychology Today. Accessed January 24, 2019. www.psychologytoday.com/us/blog/brainsnacks/201709/have-you-experienced-eureka-moments.

Hayward, Simon J. *Connected Leadership: How to Build a More Agile, Customer-driven Business.* Harlow: Pearson Education, 2016.

John P. Kotter, et al. *HBRs 10 Must Reads on Change Management.* Boston, MA: Harvard Business Review Press, 2011.

Hesselbein, Frances, and Marshall Goldsmith. *The Leader of the Future 2: Visions, Strategies, and Practices for the New Era.* San Francisco, CA: Jossey-Bass, 2006.

Hino, Satoshi. *Inside the Mind of Toyota: Management Principles for Enduring Growth.* New York: Productivity Press, 2008.

Hounshell, David A. "The Same Old Principles in the New Manufacturing. Harvard Business Review. August 01, 2014. Accessed January 26, 2019. https://hbr.org/1988/11/the-same-old-principles-in-the-new-manufacturing.

"How Caterpillars Gruesomely Transform into Butterflies. ZME Science. January 22, 2018. Accessed January 26, 2019. www.zmescience.com/ecology/animals-ecology/how-caterpillar-turn-butterfly-0534534/.

"How Do You Change a Paradigm? Moonsong. Accessed December 27, 2018. www.moonsong.com.au/how-do-you-change-a-paradigm/.

"How to Change a Paradigm". Proctor Gallagher Institute. May 14, 2018. Accessed December 27, 2018. www.proctorgallagherinstitute.com/6104/how-to-change-a-paradigm.

Ian. "Walt Disney Dreams - Curiosity, Confidence, Courage & Constancy. Challenging Coaching. September 25, 2012. Accessed January 24, 2019. https://challengingcoaching.co.uk/disney-dreams/.

"Immanuel Kant: What Is Enlightenment? (1784). Philosophical Explorations. October 02, 2013. Accessed December 27, 2018. http://braungardt.trialectics.com/philosophy/early-modern-philosophy-16th-18th-century-europe/kant/enlightenment/.

"Immanuel Kant: What Is Enlightenment? (1784). Philosophical Explorations. October 02, 2013. Accessed January 13, 2019. http://braungardt.trialectics.com/philosophy/early-modern-philosophy-16th-18th-century-europe/kant/enlightenment/.

Kahneman, Daniel. *Thinking, Fast and Slow.* New York: Farrar, Straus and Giroux, 2015.

Kaufman, Scott Barry. "The Real Neuroscience of Creativity. Scientific American Blog Network. August 19, 2013. Accessed January 24, 2019. https://blogs.scientificamerican.com/beautiful-minds/the-real-neuroscience-of-creativity/.

Keckley, Paul. "THE KECKLEY REPORT". Eroding Trust in the U.S. System Is Opportunistic for Disruptors. Accessed January 02, 2019. www.paulkeckley.com/the-keckley-report.

Klein, Janice A. *True Change.* Place of Publication Not Identified: John Wiley & Sons, 2015.

"Kolb Experiential Learning Cycle. Cognitive Learning Strategies | Wentworth Institute of Technology. January 03, 2019. Accessed December 27, 2018. https://wit.edu/lit/engage/kolb-cycle.

Krogh, George Von, Kazuo Ichijō, and Ikujirō Nonaka. *Enabling Knowledge Creation How to Unlock the Mystery of Tacit Knowledge and Release the Power of Innovation.* Oxford: Oxford University Press, 2000.

"Kyle Holland. Kaizen News - Kaizen Supplies - Kaizen Products and Books. September 17, 2013. Accessed January 26, 2019. www.kaizen-news.com/eight-steps-practical-problem-solving/.

"The Ladder of Inference: Why We Jump to Conclusions (and How to Avoid It) Synergy Commons. April 19, 2017. Accessed January 13, 2019. https://synergycommons.net/resources/the-ladder-of-inference/.

Landscape Diagram. Accessed January 02, 2019. www.hsdinstitute.org/resources/four-principles-of-change-in-human-systems-change-at-a-global-level-blog.html.

Larry, R., Sall Frani, and Doc Crouch. "High Middle Ages. The Great Courses. January 20, 2019. Accessed January 26, 2019. www.thegreatcourses.com/courses/high-middle-ages.html.

"Leader-Member Exchange (LMX) Theory. Changingminds.org. Accessed January 24, 2019. http://changingminds.org/explanations/theories/leader_member_exchange.htm.

Leadership, Cortex. YouTube. November 11, 2016. Accessed January 13, 2019. www.youtube.com/watch?v=D3APg18CZ8E.

"Learner's Path QUICKpage. Learner's Path QUICKpage. Accessed January 26, 2019. http://learnerspath.com/.

Leroy, and Donnchad. "The Hidden Factor: Why Thinking Differently Is Your Greatest Asset. The Great Courses. October 03, 2018. Accessed December 28, 2018. www.thegreatcourses.com/courses/the-hidden-factor-why-thinking-differently-is-your-greatest-asset.html.

Liker, Jeffrey K. *The Toyota Way*. New York: McGraw-Hill, 2004.

Liker, Jeffrey K., and Gary L. Convis. *The Toyota Way to Lean Leadership: Achieving and Sustaining Excellence through Leadership Development*. New York: McGraw-Hill, 2012.

Liker, Jeffrey K., and David Meier. *The Toyota Way Fieldbook a Practical Guide for Implementing Toyotas 4Ps*. New York: McGraw-Hill, 2006.

"Living in a Fast-Paced World - New-era - Lds.org. Accessed January 24, 2019. www.lds.org/new-era/2015/06/living-in-a-fast-paced-world.

"LIVING POSTMODERNISM: The Complex Balance of Worldview and ... Accessed January 24, 2019. www.growthedgecoaching.com/site/uploads/berger-ReVision-final.pdf.

Luckmanleadershipinitiative. "Luckman Leadership Initiative. Luckman Leadership Initiative. Accessed December 27, 2018. https://luckmanleadershipinitiative.word press.com/.

Lunenberg, Fred C. "Mechanistic-Organic An Axiomatic Theory. www.nationalforum.com. November 1, 2012. Accessed June 20, 2018. www.nationalforum.com/Electronic JournalVolumes/Lunenburg,FredC.MechanisticOrganicOrganizationsIJSAIDV14N 12012.pdf.

Macarthur, John. *Book on Leadership*. Place of Publication Not Identified: Thomas Nelson, 2006.

"Mapping to See: Value-Stream Improvement Workshop". Lean.org. Accessed January 26, 2019. www.lean.org/Bookstore/ProductDetails.cfm?SelectedProductId=162.

Maxwell, John C. *The Five Levels of Leadership:|bproven Steps to Maximize Your Potential*. New York: Center Street, 2011.

Maxwell, John C. *How Successful People Think: Change Your Thinking, Change Your Life*. New York: Center Street, 2016.

Maxwell, John C. *The 21 Irrefutable Laws of Leadership: Follow Them and People Will Follow You*. Nashville, TN: Thomas Nelson, 1998, 2007.

McKee, Annie, Joel Garfinkle, Amit Maimon, and Ron Ashkenas. "A 3-Step Process to Break a Cycle of Frustration, Stress, and Fighting at Work". Harvard Business

Review. November 29, 2017. Accessed January 26, 2019. https://hbr.org/2017/07/a-3-step-process-to-break-a-cycle-of-frustration-stress-and-fighting-at-work.

Meadows, Donella. "Leverage Points. Sustainability Institute. December 1999. Accessed December 22, 2018. www.donellameadows.org/wp-content/userfiles/Leverage_Points.pdf.

Meadows, Donella H., and Diana Wright. *Thinking in Systems: A Primer*. White River Junction, VT: Chelsea Green Publishing, 2015.

"Metamorphosis. Dictionary.com. Accessed January 24, 2019. www.dictionary.com/browse/metamorphosis.

Miller, John H., and Scott E. Page. *Complex Adaptive Systems: An Introduction to Computational Models of Social Life*. Princeton, NJ: Princeton University Press, 2007.

Mitchell, Melanie. *Complexity: A Guided Tour*. New York: Oxford University Press, 2011.

"The Modern Intellectual Tradition: From Descartes to … Accessed December 26, 2018. www.thegreatcourses.com/courses/modern-intellectual-tradition-from-descartes-to-derrida.html.

Moeller, Kathryn, and Kathryn Moeller. "The Ghost Statistic That Haunts Women's Empowerment." *The New Yorker*, January 14, 2019, www.newyorker.com/science/elements/the-ghost-statistic-that-haunts-womens-empowerment

Moen, Ronald. "Foundation and History of the PDSA Cycle. PDSA History. Accessed December 18, 2018. https://deming.org/uploads/paper/PDSA_History_Ron_Moen.pdf.

Moore, Harold G., and Mike Guardia. *Hal Moore on Leadership: Winning When Outgunned and Outmanned*. Maple Grove, MN: Magnum Books, 2017.

"MSG Management Study Guide. Kotter's 8 Step Model of Change. Accessed January 24, 2019. www.managementstudyguide.com/transformational-leadership.htm.

"Neuroscience for Leadership". E-Book Download PDF. Accessed January 24, 2019. www.e-bookdownload.net/search/neuroscience-for-leadership.

"The Neuroscience of Trust. Psychology Today. Accessed January 13, 2019. www.psychologytoday.com/us/blog/the-athletes-way/201508/the-neuroscience-trust.

Nevis, Edwin, Joan E. Lancourt, and Helen G. Vassallo. *Implementing Transformational Change: Strategies for the Practitioner*. San Francisco, CA: Jossey-Bass, 1996.

Nevis, Sonia March, and Joseph Melnick. *The Evolution of the Cape Cod Model*. Gestalt Institute Study Center Press, 2018.

O'Toole, Warren Bennis James. "How Business Schools Lost Their Way. Harvard Business Review. August 01, 2014. Accessed January 02, 2019. https://hbr.org/2005/05/how-business-schools-lost-their-way.

Obolensky, Nick. *Complex Adaptive Leadership Embracing Paradox and Uncertainty*. Milton: Routledge, 2017.

Olson, Edwin E., and Glenda H. Eoyang. *Facilitating Organizational Change: Lessons from Complexity Science*. San Francisco, CA: Jossey-Bass, 2001.

"Overcoming Defensive Routines in the Workplace. The Systems Thinker. April 25, 2017. Accessed January 02, 2019. https://thesystemsthinker.com/overcoming-defensive-routines-in-the-workplace/.

Padgett, John Frederick, and Walter W. Powell. *The Emergence of Organizations and Markets*. Princeton, NJ: Princeton University Press, 2012.

"Paradigm Change". Definition of Sustainability. Accessed December 27, 2018. www.thwink.org/sustain/glossary/ParadigmChange.htm.

Pascale, Richard T., Mark Milleman, and Linda Gioja. *Surfing the Edge of Chaos: The Laws of Nature and the New Laws of Business*. New York: Crown Publishers, 2000.

"Perfecting Patient Journeys. Lean.org. Accessed January 26, 2019. www.lean.org/ppj.

Phillips, Donald/ Runger Nelson (Nrt). *Lincoln on Leadership*. New York:Warner Books Inc., 2000.

"Quest for Meaning: Values, Ethics, and the Modern Experience. Accessed December 26, 2018. www.thegreatcourses.com/courses/quest-for-meaning-values-ethics-and-the-modern-experience.html.

Richardson, Tracey M., and Ernie Richardson. *The Toyota Engagement Equation: How to Understand and Implement Continuous Improvement Thinking in Any Organization*. New York: McGraw-Hill, 2017.

RJP2. "Masters of Mindfulness: Transforming Your Mind and Body. The Great Courses. December 26, 2018. Accessed January 02, 2019. www.thegreatcourses.com/courses/masters-of-mindfulness-transforming-your-mind-and-body.html.

Rock, David. *Quiet Leadership: Six Steps to Transforming Performance at Work; Help People Think Better – Dont Tell Them What to Do!*. New York: HarperCollins, 2006.

Rock, David, and Linda J. Page. *Coaching with the Brain in Mind: Foundations for Practice*. Hoboken, NJ: Wiley, 2009.

"The Role of Leadership Style in Employee Engagement. Accessed January 24, 2019. http://digitalcommons.fiu.edu/cgi/viewcontent.cgi?article=1143&context=sferc.

Schein, Edgar H. *Process Consultation Revisited: Building the Helping Relationship*. Reading, MA: Addison Wesley, 2008.

Schein, Edgar H. *Humble Inquiry: The Gentle Art of Asking Instead of Telling*. San Francisco, CA: Berrett-Koehler Publishers, 2014.

"Science Fiction Writers Workshop: Joseph Campbell's Hero's Journey. Joseph Campbell's 'The Hero's Journey' Materials. Accessed January 26, 2019. www.sfcenter.ku.edu/Workshop-stuff/Joseph-Campbell-Hero-Journey.htm.

Sellers, Clay. "What Are You Willing to Let Go - To Grow. Saybrook.typepad.com. October 13, 2011. Accessed December 28, 2012. https://saybrook.typepad.com/complexity/2011/10/what-are-you-willing-t/.

Shift the Paradigm". Shift the Paradigm. Accessed December 27, 2018. https://1paradigm.org/.

Shook, John, and James P. Womack. *Managing to Learn: Using the A3 Management Process to Solve Problems, Gain Agreement, Mentor and Lead*. Cambridge, MA: Lean Enterprise Institute, 2010.

Siminovitch, Dorothy E. *A Gestalt Coaching Primer*. Toronto: Gestalt Coaching Works, LLC, 2017.

"Simple vs. Complicated vs. Complex vs. Chaotic. NOOP.NL. August 20, 2008. Accessed December 28, 2018. http://noop.nl/2008/08/simple-vs-complicated-vs-complex-vs-chaotic.html.

Simpson, Michael K. *Unlocking Potential: 7 Coaching Skills That Transform Individuals, Teams & Organizations*. Chennai: Grand Harbor Press, 2018.

Sinek, Simon. *Start with Why: How Great Leaders Inspire Everyone to Take Action*. London: Portfolio/Penguin, 2013.

Sinek, Simon. *Leaders Eat Last*. Place of Publication Not Identified: Portfolio/Penguin, 2018.

Snyder, Karolyn J., Michele Acker-Hocevar, and Kristen M. Snyder. *Living on the Edge of Chaos: Leading Schools into the Global Age*. Milwaukee, WI: ASQ Quality Press, 2008.

Social Media and the Speed of Communication. Accessed January 24, 2019. www. tributemedia.com/blog/social-media-and-the-speed-of-communication.

"Soft Systems Methodology in Action: Peter Checkland, Jim … Accessed January 25, 2019. www.amazon.com/Systems-Methodology-Action-Peter-Checkland/dp/ 0471986054.

Sol, Mateo, and Aletheia Luna. "The Spiritual Awakening Process - Kindle Edition by Mateo Sol, Aletheia Luna. Religion & Spirituality Kindle EBooks @ Amazon.com. Amazon. Accessed January 24, 2019. www.amazon.com/Spiritual-Awakening-Pro cess-Mateo-Sol-ebook/dp/B01M6WBEZI.

Soman, Ebey. "Summary of Immanuel Kant's Enlightenment. Owlcation. January 12, 2018a. Accessed December 27, 2018. https://owlcation.com/humanities/Summary-of-Immanuel-Kants-Enlightenment.

Soman, Ebey. "Summary of Immanuel Kant's Enlightenment. Owlcation. January 12, 2018b. Accessed January 13, 2019. https://owlcation.com/humanities/Summary-of-Immanuel-Kants-Enlightenment.

Stacey, Ralph D., and Chris Mowles. *Strategic Management and Organisational Dynamics: The Challenge of Complexity to Ways of Thinking about Organisations.* Harlow: Pearson Education, 2016.

Sterling, Dianna. "Learning and Complex Adaptive Systems. Learning-CAS. Accessed May 31, 2014. www.learndev.org/dl/Stirling_Learning-CAS.pdf.

Stroh, David Peter. *Systems Thinking for Social Change: A Practical Guide to Solving Complex Problems, Avoiding Unintended Consequences, and Achieving Lasting Results.* White River Junction, VT: Chelsea Green Publishing, 2015.

Tandon, Kamakshi. "Roger Federer Credits Switch to Bigger Racquet for Improved Backhand". Accessed October 16, 2018. www.tennis.com/pro-game/2017/03/ roger-federer-racquet-change-backhand-rafael-nadal-indian-wells/64840/

Tierney, William G., and Edgar H. Schein. "Organizational Culture and Leadership". *The Academy of Management Review* 11, no. 3 (1986): 677. doi:10.2307/258322.

"Toyota Global Site | Customer First Spirit Delivers Quality. Accessed February 2, 2016. www.toyota-global.com/company/toyota_traditions/philosophy/mar_sep_2010. html.

"Trust Factor: The Key to High Performance with Paul Zak. Roger Dooley. February 01, 2017. Accessed January 13, 2019. www.rogerdooley.com/key-high-performance-paul-zak.

Ukko, Adele. "Quest for Meaning: Values, Ethics, and the Modern Experience. The Great Courses. September 18, 2018. Accessed February/March, 2016. www.thegreat courses.com/courses/quest-for-meaning-values-ethics-and-the-modern-experience. html.

"What Is Transactional Leadership? How Structure Leads to Results. St. Thomas University Online. November 25, 2014. Accessed January 24, 2019. https://online.stu. edu/articles/education/what-is-transactional-leadership.aspx.

"What Psychological Safety Is Not – The IAOM. Accessed January 13, 2019. www. theiaom.org/what-psychological-safety-is-not/.

Wirth, Claus-Peter., and Thomas S. Kuhn. *The Structure of Scientific Revolutions: Zweisprachige Auszüge Mit Deutschem Kommentar.* Saarbrücken: Univ., Fachrichtung Informatik, 2007.

Womack, James P., and Daniel T. Jones. *Lean Thinking: Banish Waste and Create Wealth in Your Corporation.* Riverside, CA: Free Press, 2010.

Wooden, John R., and Steve Jamison. *Wooden on Leadership*. New York: McGraw-Hill, 2005.

Yunus, Muhammad. Accessed January 26, 2019. https://grameenfoundation.org/about/history.

Zak, Paul J. "The Neuroscience of Trust. Harvard Business Review. December 19, 2016. Accessed January 13, 2019. https://hbr.org/2017/01/the-neuroscience-of-trust.

Index

value-stream metrics, 79
value-stream perspective, 83
value-stream problems, xix, 74, 79, 81, 88,
    123, 132
value-stream thinking, 78–79, 88
Verble, David, 96
vertical organization, 77

W

Ward, Alan, 20, 109
Washington, George, 50

Welch, Jack, 8–9, 166, 178
Wiio, Osmo A., 93
Womack, James P., xvi, 183–184
Wooden, John, 185

Y

Yunus, Muhammad, 33–34, 185

Z

Zak, Paul J., 94, 184–185

Printed in the United States
by Baker & Taylor Publisher Services